The
Visual
Elements
of
Landscape

The
Visual
Elements
of
Landscape

John A. Jakle

The University of Massachusetts Press

Amherst, 1987

Copyright © 1987 by The University of Massachusetts Press
All rights reserved
Printed in the United States of America
Typeset in Linoterm Bembo at The University of Massachusetts Press
Printed by Thomson-Shore and bound by John H. Dekker and Sons, Inc.

Library of Congress Cataloging-in-Publication Data

Jakle, John A.
  The visual elements of landscape.

  Bibliography: p.
  Includes index.
   1. Landscape assessment. 2. Geographical perception.
I. Title.
GF90.J35   1987   710   86–25078
ISBN 0–87023–566–4 (alk. paper)
ISBN 0–87023–567–2 (pbk. : alk. paper)

For Cynthia

Contents

Preface

Landscape (the environment that surrounds us) is a multi-faceted thing. In this book I emphasize only its visual aspect. I ask: What attracts the eye in the visual world? What do people tend to see when they encounter their surroundings? I do not intend this to be a treatise on how to look at landscape. To write such a book would entail interpreting the built environment as cultural and social history. It would entail concern with the economic and political functioning of places. It would necessitate understanding physical and biological systems implicit in natural processes. Instead, I mean to focus on seeing landscape as visual display. My concern, highly restricted as it is, is neither the logical beginning place nor the ultimate ending place of landscape study. It is merely one dimension of landscape appreciation, albeit an important dimension that deserves renewed emphasis and increased comprehension.

Many students of cultural landscape (the surrounding built

environment) shy away from aesthetics, visual or otherwise. In founding *Landscape,* the journal dedicated to landscape interpretation, J. B. Jackson took as a guiding principle the notion that landscapes were to be read and interpreted according to function rather than merely appraised visually.[1] Mere seeing was deemed less important than understanding landscapes as lived-in places. Real comprehension grew from awareness of function in the identification of cultural, social, economic, and political contexts. This is clearly the view of the American mainstream wherein utilitarian values are seen to dominate life's experiencing. Such emphasis has proven overly restrictive. Ignored have been the aesthetic values of the picturesque. Some places—parks and gardens, for instance—are intended to be beautiful, and being beautiful is their function. These kinds of places certainly demand concern with landscape visualization.

Concern with seeing is needed to comprehend all landscapes, and not just those intended to be picturesque. Landscapes function as centers of human intent. Places nest in landscapes as settings of behavioral predisposition, guiding behavior according to their appearance and structuring. For people who are sighted, places are first known for their appearances. Expectations and, indeed, ongoing human activities flow from this seeing as inclinations to act are cued visually. To ignore how places communicate visually is to eclipse the functional interpretation of landscape. My concern with the visual elements of landscape is not intended to portend rejection of the current emphasis on utility. I seek to amplify the functional interpretation of cultural landscape by incorporating in it a clear visual dimension. It is time to bring a sense for the picturesque more into the mainstream of cultural landscape analysis.

Most students of the built environment have focused on landscape as object reality. Scientism, as a basic value system, has influenced both social scientists and humanists in this regard. But the subject of landscape as it appears to be (not as it actually is) is, to me, as important for those concerned with comprehending human behavior as are the realities of landscape established through presumed objective observation. What people think they see in a landscape, and not the actual structure of landscape per se, influences how they behave in it.

Thus this book is intended for scholars with an abiding interest in images, especially in the images of place around which people's conceptualization of the world as habitat derives. I focus on place images rooted in peoples' seeing of landscape, believing as I do that there are abstract visual elements in landscape to be defined above and beyond normative comprehensions of function and form.

This book represents a personal journey undertaken in the tradition of the humanities. It began as an attempt to understand my seeing the world as a visual display. It broadened into an endeavor to comprehend other people's seeing of landscapes. Herein, I share my discoveries both through photographs and in narrative. The photographs are central because they not only display the profound variety of potential visual interest to be discovered in cultural landscape, but they also demonstrate the pictorial conventions whereby landscapes may be pictured. In the narrative I offer a synthesis of a wide-ranging literature on landscape visualization. I seek to communicate about my seeing by examining the words others have used to describe their seeing, with the objectives of promoting a shared vocabulary for visualizing landscape and assembling basic concepts whereby landscape visualization may be better understood and discussed.

What follows is not a scientific treatise, although it relies, in part, on the insights of psychologists and others who do operate in scientific modes. Neither is it a treatise on design, although it relies upon the creative insights of architects, landscape architects, and other designers. The book represents the effort of one person to comprehend what attracts the eye in the visual environment. I proceed in the belief that we human beings can still learn much about ourselves by examining our own experiences of being in the world. I do not pretend to establish definitive truths regarding how people see their surroundings, nor is it my intent to answer questions so much as it is to ask them.

As I cut across the intellectual territories of many academic disciplines, I serve none of the established literatures directly. Although my instincts are rooted with J. B. Jackson and today's cultural landscape "school" as anchored in academic cultural geography, my intent is to reach beyond to draw diverse threads into a rather different fabric of landscape concern. My intent is to synthesize: to borrow from many sources of insight with the goal of discovering new common ground. Specifically, I focus on defining basic concepts describing the visual world around us. Mine is a search for the visual elements of landscape, defining these elements both photographically and verbally. Mine is a personal return to the experiential base of laity seeing landscape. It is not an attempt to summarize all that specialists have written from their various points of view. It is, instead, one person's point of view calculated to excite a line of questioning both fresh and revealing.

My work advocates rediscovery of an early use of the term *landscape:* a verbal artifact of European landscape painting. Such words as *landschaft, landskip,* and *landscape* were first used in German, Dutch, and English to describe visual environment depicted by artists. Subsequently, geographers and other scholars came to use the term to indicate that which was depicted rather than the depiction itself. Landscapes considered as concrete objects came to be valued for the utilities manifest in their structuring.[2] I would emphasize more the original intent of the word. Again, I do so not to exclude function and structure as analytical concerns, but to broaden understanding of the geographical environment as a container of human behavior: behavior rooted in people's use of place images, especially visual images.

Photographs are intended to illustrate each of the principal elements of landscape described. They depict both urban and rural places. Although the concepts defined herein apply to all kinds of settings, I do emphasize urban scenes in a focus on environments clearly built by humankind. The scenes depicted are from the United States, Great Britain, and Canada. They are deliberately mixed to heighten focus on the concepts rather than on the places depicted. The diversity of places used in illustration reflects the universality of the concepts, for they describe the visual relationships between landscape components applicable literally everywhere. I have chosen visual images familiar to an English-speaking readership because I want readers to apply the concepts defined here to their experiences of familiar places.

In order to grasp the subject matter of landscape visualization, I focus attention on sightseeing, which I define as the spontaneous visual assessment of landscape as, for example, when tourists seek visual pleasure in travel. Sightseeing involves role playing whereby sightseers actively engage their environments as visual display. Landscape visualization is important to all human activity, but only as a sightseer, I feel, does a person act deliberately to find visual satisfaction. In this book, therefore, I emphasize the quest for landscape as scenery. It has been argued that the search for universals in landscape attractiveness is futile: that the quest for scenery cannot be separated from the many other life pursuits that give landscape meaning. Landscapes, it has been said, cannot be assessed like works of art.[3] I disagree and think that, quite to the contrary, people in certain circumstances do seek visual encounters with landscape to the exclusion of other pursuits and that those encounters can be very much like encounters with art objects, especially the pictorial art of pictures and the graphical art of maps.

In outline, I have chosen to organize my thoughts as follows. Chapter 1 presents a range of questions students of landscape visualization might pursue, focusing on the sightseer and sightseeing. Chapter 2 concerns the process of visualization, relating key notions about "place" and "space" to the act of viewing the visual environment, whereas chapter 3 focuses on the search for "prospect" and "refuge" as basic dimensions of landscape visualization. Chapter 4 concerns the details of landscape which give character to place; chapter 5 focuses on landscape as pictorial composition; and chapter 6 relates the pictorial aspects of landscape visualization to the processes of cognitive mapping whereby a sense of geography obtains. Chapter 7 offers concluding observations as encouragement to future research on landscape visualization linked to design.

The
Visual
Elements
of
Landscape

Chapter 1

Introduction

The beauty of life is involved very largely with the outline of its scenery.

THEODORE DREISER

Most students of cultural landscape focus on objects in the built environment, both individual structures and clusters of structures defined as settlement forms. Form is usually seen to follow from function both in the static sense of utility manifest in objects at a single point in time, and in the dynamic sense of utility evolving over time in changing forms. Such emphases undoubtedly follow the layperson's tendency to see function in landscape, often to the exclusion of other characteristics of place. Objects are seen and given meaning primarily for their anticipated use. Rarely is the seeing of things, in and of itself, an essential concern.

The visualization of landscape has been taken very much for granted in this emphasis on utility. That various people might see and thus define elements of a landscape variously, or that the same person might see the same landscape differently, even in similar circumstances, has received serious attention only recently. Geographer Edward Relph notes: "Within one

3

person the mixing of experience, emotion, memory, imagination, present situation, and intention can be so variable that he can see a particular place in several quite distinct ways."[1] What then do people see in landscape? What meanings, functional or otherwise, do they assign? How are the meaningful objects and object clusters of one's surroundings conceptualized on the basis of visual experience? These sorts of questions beg a new orientation to an old subject. This essay is intended to explore concepts basic to that reorientation.

Place is a concept fundamental to the study of landscape. The concept serves to link concern with structure in landscape to human behavior. A place is a setting that, because it contains a distinctive range of social interactions, may be thought of as inviting or inducing the continuation of those interactions. A place retains its meaning to the extent that people continue to expect certain satisfactions (or dissatisfactions) implicit in behaviors contained. Despite its fundamental nature and its implicit value to geographical scholarship, the place concept has received relatively little attention. Geographer Yi-Fu Tuan notes: "We live, act and orient ourselves in a world that is richly and profoundly differentiated into places, yet at the same time we seem to have a meagre understanding of the constitution of places and the ways in which we experience them."[2]

The process of selecting among alternative places in order to pursue a specific behavior is the essence of what geographers call human spatial behavior. Traditionally, geographers have been preoccupied with the locational aspects of place selection and thus have preferred the adjective *spatial* to describe their research. The adjective *place-seeking* or even newly contrived words, such as *place-specific* or *platial* (as in *platial behavior*) are in my opinion more appropriate. Location is merely one criterion by which places are known and selected as settings for intended activity. For Relph, location or position is neither a necessary nor a sufficient condition of place, even if it is a very common condition. He writes: "Location in the strict cartographic sense is merely an incidental quality of place."[3]

Concern with landscape visualization necessarily begins with the idea of place and explores the manner by which different kinds of places are identified by different kinds of people in search of various sorts of satisfaction. Certainly, places, as behavioral settings, have spatial context. They also, however,

Figures 1.1 and 1.2

Places as behavioral settings—
Victoria, British Columbia, and
Buffalo, New York. Study of
visual landscape begins with the
concept of place. Places are
behavioral settings linked to
anticipated satisfactions and
dissatisfactions. Place meanings
are variously cued by location and
point in time, and by their
occupants, their activities, and
the objects they use, including
signs. Places link to one another
through implications of use.

have temporal dimension because they open and close at set
points in time and thus function for set durations of time, often
with cyclical regularity. They are occupied by people (usually
a limited range of types), by activities (usually a limited set of
general behaviors), and by a limited array of furnishings supportive of those behaviors. Thus places are situations in space
and time anticipated according to ongoing behaviors as defined
by actors, their activities, and the props supportive of those
activities. Meanings are attached to places according to the
expectations people develop in their repeated rounds of place
encounter.[4]

Figure 1.1 illustrates the place concept. Two advertising
"sandwich boards" are paraded along a public sidewalk creat-

Figures 1.3 and 1.4
Places defined at different
scales—Bethlehem,
Pennsylvania, and Bath,
England. Places nest in landscape
at varying scales. Here a
neighborhood, a street, a
building, and even a folding chair
carry distinctive place meanings.
All places communicate their
function: some overtly, as the
street in Bethlehem, and some
covertly, as at the cricket ground
in Bath. Students of landscape
must be concerned with place
definitions at all scales if they are
to comprehend landscape as
visual environment.

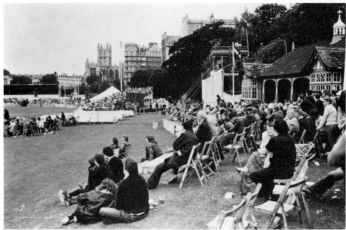

ing a social situation with only ephemeral place implication.
A passerby turns to appreciate the scene because the women, in
their novel context, create a presence that attracts. They have
been hired to promote place usage at a distance, to develop
awarenesses and expectations relative to other places. This
moment in space and time, signified by a limited set of activities and built around an unusual set of props defines for the
passerby a clear sense of place if only for the instant. Figure 1.2
pictures a delicatessen, the kind of place a sandwich board
might advertise. This place is permanently structured toward
encouraging a range of expected activities. The store is clearly
bounded, linked inside and out by a carefully configured

entrance surrounded by display windows and an overhead sign. The windows serve to snare pedestrians and the sign flags the store for motorists. Here is a stable setting toward which behavior may be indefinitely directed.

The street at Bethlehem, Pennsylvania, takes on different place meanings for the tourist searching for a meal or a bed for the night, for the shopper seeking out specific merchandise, for the commuter journeying to a distant workplace or returning home (fig. 1.3). Places nest at various scales of conceptualization: the city as a whole laid out below the hill, the street itself as a way of passage, stores and houses as landmarks in passing or even as potential destinations. At the cricket ground at Bath, England, people assume suitable places in order to play the game, to cheer close at hand, to watch respectfully from a distance (fig. 1.4). The place breaks down into settings conducive to different kinds of behavior, all interrelated and mutually self-supporting.

Places nest in landscape according to viewer intentions. Each individual defines a different set of relevant places based on anticipated behavior. Thus architect John Donat writes: "Places occur at all levels of identity, my place, your place, street, community, town, county, region, country, and continent, but places never conform to tidy hierarchies of classification. They all overlap and interpenetrate one another and are wide open to a variety of interpretation."[5] Generally, people focus on the settings or situations relevant to the needs at hand, ignoring all others. This profound notion that place meaning shifts with behavioral intent has, probably more than any other fact, discouraged geographers and others from operationalizing the place concept in research design. Whose cognition are we to study? Which behavioral motivations are most significant?

Places are cued visually. Tuan states: "Place is whatever stable object catches our attention." As the individual searches the landscape, places are discerned as loci of meaning purposeful in the specific behavioral context. Architect Christian Norberg-Schultz sees place as "totality made up of concrete things having material substance, shape, texture, and colour." Together these things determine an "environmental character" which is the "essence of place." What then are the meaningful place cues reflective of different kinds of behavior, different motivations, different sorts of satisfaction? How are places cued under various circumstances? If answers can be given to such questions, an important step will have been taken toward comprehending the built environment, not simply as a set of functionally given forms, but as a system of symbols predisposing or otherwise influencing behavior.[6]

Architect Amos Rapoport thinks of places as eliciting place-appropriate behaviors. Certainly, places cue meanings which when placed in the context of an on-going behavior can encourage limited behavioral response. Thus the visual environment, broken into place-specific categories of meaning, can be seen to contain symbolic information. Although long a cliché, the old adage that every landscape represents a "to whom it may concern message" bears repeating here. Landscapes comprise a syntax.[7] Not only do objects have meaning like words, but objects relate spatially not unlike a grammatical structure. Objects in the environment can have collective meaning given the visual relationships of place. But how might visual environment be altered to enhance such communication? How can places be made imageable?

FOCUS ON TOURISTIC BEHAVIOR

The tourist is, I believe, the most logical kind of person upon whom to focus the initial study of landscape visualization. Of all the varied kinds of general activity, tourism, more than any other, involves the deliberate searching out of place experience. Searching the landscape visually for place cues is an overt, deliberate preoccupation of pleasure tripping. Sightseeing is of the essence in tourism. It is not just an interesting aside significant because all behavior is necessarily landscape contained. The commuter in the journey-to-work, the shopper in the journey-to-shop, also visualize landscape in making travel decisions. But only for the sightseer is the search for unique place experience the primary motivation for travel. Tuan writes of tourists:

> In our mobile society the fleeting impressions of people passing through cannot be neglected. Generally speaking, we may say that only the visitor (and particularly the tourist) has a viewpoint; his perception is often a matter of using his eyes to compose pic-

tures. The native, by contrast, has a complex attitude derived from his immersion in the totality of his environment. The visitor's viewpoint, being simple, is easily stated. The complex attitude of the native, on the other hand, can be expressed by him only with difficulty.[8]

Thus a first order of concern regarding the visual experiencing of landscape is to ask: What does the sightseer see in landscape? What meanings get attached to place accordingly?

Scholars have traditionally avoided the study of tourism except insofar as tourism has demonstrated an impact on land use or local economy or both in a "form follows function" sort of view. Written accounts of travel experience have been discounted as being superficial, reflecting as they do conditioned responses to landscape encoded in culture and society. Admittedly, tourism does lead to superficial understandings about places. It does involve stereotyped behavior. But those very characteristics make tourism, and especially its sightseeing aspect, all the more appropriate to the initial study of how people comprehend visual environment. The tourist's responses to place are usually superficial (if not simplistic) and, therefore, readily identified and studied.

Tourism, despite its superficialities, is far from unimportant. To the contrary, it is a vital activity in societies characterized by extensive geographical mobility and substantial leisure time. Travel for pleasure not only relieves the tensions of highly pressurized modern life, but, more important, as sociologist Dean MacCannell argues, tourism is a major means by which modern man relates to society at large. As a worker, the individual's relationship to society is partial and limited, secured by a fragile "work ethic," and restricted to a single position among millions in the division of labor. But as a tourist, the individual may step into the "universal drama of modernity" and grasp "the division of labor as a phenomenon *sui generis*."[9] Society, particularized and formalized through the specializations and segregations of workshop and residence, can no longer be comprehended in its complexity. Modern people depend upon the media of the popular culture and formal education to glimpse society in its totality and assign themselves identity within. But the media and the schools are contrived. Only seeing firsthand under conditions

Figure 1.5

Tourist attraction—the Alamo at San Antonio, Texas. Tourism is focused at places specially contrived as visual displays. Distinctive role playing is encouraged, including taking snapshots intended to preserve place experience in memory. The mission's facade, visible across a large open space enframed by trees, makes it easy for visitors not only to see, but also to remember the Alamo.

of informality and spontaneity produces understandings of real trust. A tourist may obtain only superficial comprehensions, but they are comprehensions of his own making and they can be believed accordingly. Tourism provides the opportunity to see for oneself, to validate firsthand the world and one's role in it.

Most tourist travel involves seeking out places specially contrived for enjoyment: resorts, parks, museums, displays of various kinds. Who can resist seeking out the Alamo in a visit to San Antonio (fig. 1.5)? Here is an attraction physically contrived to honor a historical event vital to the Texan sense of identity. Almost obligatory is a snapshot recording the visit. Through photographs the tourist verifies the fact of place experience. Indeed, for many tourists, attractions are experienced primarily through the viewfinder of a camera in a search for pictures. Inserting one's companions or oneself into a photograph amplifies the sense of personal association. The Alamo is configured to accommodate the visitor whose experiences are constrained toward set comprehensions implicit in set displays.

The pleasure trip is a linking of contrived attractions in a circuit out and back from one's home. However, the sightseeing that I will focus on in this book involves the stretches between such places where the traveler can relate spontaneously to landscape as an unwinding visual display of place stimulation. It might be a rural or wilder landscape viewed

Figure 1.6

Spontaneous sightseeing—
Gastown in Vancouver, British
Columbia. The sightseeing most
significant in the study of
landscape visualization is
illustrated here. Spontaneous
sightseeing leaves sightseers free
to selectively explore their visual
environment relatively free of
touristic contrivances.
Sightseeing involves movement
in search of visual pleasure
directed but not tyrannized by the
structuring of space.

from a highway in a speeding car. Or it might be a streetscape in a town or city as a traveler ambles on foot toward some destination. Such spontaneous sightseeing, in my opinion, offers the most appropriate circumstance for beginning the study of the visual experience of place. As tourists rather than natives, people scan the landscape with fresh eyes and a reduced sense of behavioral expectation. Tourists come as strangers with accompanying needs to orient to new places. What they see is novel and it attracts attention accordingly. As they seek interest and pleasure in their visual surroundings, they are sensitive to those aspects of landscape, to those places, which portend interest and pleasure.

Spontaneous sightseeing can be observed wherever tourists gather, as, for example, in Vancouver's Gastown, a refurbished "historic" district replete with boutiques, restaurants, and other businesses catering to visitors (fig. 1.6). People saunter along Water Street variously attracted to specific establishments. The area's brick paving and its nostalgic streetlights and other furnishings provide visual integration, tying the whole together as a kind of place: a milieu that is more than the sum of its parts. The visitor is less programmed into set patterns of experience.

Spontaneous sightseers do not memorize landscape but move in search of scenery to bask in the flow of pleasure-giving images. Architect Niels Prak likens such sightseeing to the enjoyment of popular music. Such music is easily enjoyed because it has low information content for the experience at hand: simple melodies involving a relative few chords and many repetitions.[10] (By analogy, as study of musical signature might begin with lighter composition, so the study of landscape visualization might begin with sightseeing as a less complex form of place experience.) Only with heightened attention will tourists seek to linger and savor a sight as they might seek to remember a striking melody. They will retain such places in memory in proportion to their vividness and to the degree to which they satisfied an immediate need. Thus sightseeing is, above all, a search for stimulating views. Places of high touristic value are almost always scenic. Experiencing such places not only gives immediate pleasure, but experience remembered forms the basis of self-identity in the remembering of pleasurable circumstances. In addition, remembered sights, when shared with others in the retelling, serve to build social status. Concern with the visual experiencing of landscape, therefore, can be reduced to a consideration of scenery. The most significant place cues for sightseers are necessarily scenery related. The relevant questions become: What makes a landscape scenic? What attracts attention as a scenic place?

COPING WITH LANGUAGE

Most people are hard pressed to describe sights seen. Visualization of landscape suffers from a lack of coherent vocabulary capable of describing scenes as visually pleasurable places. Language is not indispensable to human thought, but it certainly helps. Objects in the landscape are known primarily by the words we attach. Words categorize things, indicating the level of abstractness at which an object is perceived or ought to be perceived.[11] When complex abstractions are labeled by words, the speaker's thinking maintains them more firmly. In Western society, objects and sets of objects in landscape tend to be named to reflect their function, but sets of objects as they strike distinctive visual relationships with one another tend not to be named. Stated differently, the abstract spatial relationships between objects are poorly classified. Without adequate descriptors we may not notice them or easily remember them when we do notice them.

Cues to place meaning, especially cues to the scenic places of

---

touristic interest, tend to be abstract, communicated more in a visual language of form and spatial relationship. In Western culture, form in landscape, as an aesthetic quality, has carried few functional implications except among artists, architects, and their patrons whose life interest in beauty has been to see well what most see poorly. Concern with the visual experiencing of landscape must necessarily start with the languages used to describe such comprehension. It must deal with both the visual vocabulary of landscape itself and with the verbalization used to communicate visual comprehensions. Two languages are involved: first, the abstract object relationships of the landscape and, second, the verbal forms used as descriptors or classifiers in everyday speech.

Grady Clay, student of American urban landscapes, writes of the "object-ridden" language which must be awkwardly manipulated to deal with the visual qualities of cities. He advocates a "loosening" of language. "One must relax, let the words hang loose and take up their own new and often awkward-appearing positions. And one must keep it up, fitting, comparing, and reshaping—mindful of the history of language but alert to meanings that are evolving and emerging. Neither language nor landscape stands still for us." He concludes that we must "learn to say what we see." Art historian Kenneth Clark recognizes the essentially conservative and stabilizing aspect of language in his assessment of art. He fancies that one cannot enjoy a pure aesthetic sensation for longer than a few minutes without verbal language to fix ideas and give the mind a "second wind" to allow powers of receptivity to renew. Words provide intellectual pretext, keeping the eye unconsciously engaged. Expanding language to more fully embrace the abstractions of landscape visualization would seem to be an entirely positive venture. People tend to suppress that which they cannot express. If an experience resists communication, a common response is to deem it private, even idiosyncratic, and hence unimportant. [12]

Written or spoken language by its very nature presents problems for conceptualizing landscape. Verbal experience is not the same as visual experience. People respond to space as a totality, from many directions simultaneously, but verbal thought proceeds linearly, from concept to concept. Rudolf Arnheim emphasizes verbal thinking as strings of perceptual concepts in linear succession. Verbalization cuts one-dimensional paths through the spatial landscape intellectually. He writes: "Intellectual thinking dismantles the simultaneity of spatial structure."[13] As sightseers scan a landscape, the events in their surroundings are stripped of their redundant features to expose the basic structures of spatial relationship. Some relationships are translated into verbal code and, as such, are more easily remembered, that which cannot be verbalized tending to slip from retention. What then is the language of scenic appreciation? What do sightseers say they see when they see it? Perhaps more specific to the purpose at hand, what words might sightseers use to describe what they see?

Researchers in Europe have developed the study of landscape semiosis: the study of landscape as symbol system. The constitutive elements of landscape are seen as analogous to constitutive linguistic elements or words. Architect M. Krampen observes: "There seems to be a strong tendency to think that since all languages are made up of words and all words are signs, all things made up of signs are languages." Thus the landscape is seen to stand as a language in its own right. It stands as that "to whom it may concern message" with its own syntactics (the relation of signs among themselves), semantics (the relation of signs to the objects they stand for), and pragmatics (the relation of signs to their users).[14] Thus architect Donald Preziosi defines the built environment as an "architectonic code," a system of relationships manifested in material formations.

> A glance down any street will reveal a multi-dimensional mosaic of colors, textures, shapes, sizes, and materials. But a closer look will reveal the presence of the same colors applied to differently shaped formations, or of different colors applied to identically shaped formations, or of different colors applied to identically shaped forms which are of different relative sizes. Moreover, each of these permutations may be multiplied across contrastive materials, or across contrastive textures of the same materials.[15]

What might initially have seemed a visual continuum resolves itself into a highly complex multidimensional system of contrastive oppositions cued by disjunctions both in geometry and material.

Distinctions or disjunctions in the landscape cue differences in meaning in a manner precisely analogous to other semiotic systems, such as verbal language. As a system of cues, however, the landscape is co-occurrent with ensembles of other sign systems in different media. Each sign system offers certain advantages over others under the varying circumstances of life. Preziosi writes of architectural forms: "A built environment does certain things which verbal language does not do, or only does by weak approximation and circumlocution—and vice-versa."[16] What then do sightseers see in the landscape which words poorly express, or do not express at all? What does the landscape express to them directly, and even beneath the consciousness of their verbal ability?

The chapters that follow seek to go beyond the usual preoccupations with form and function in landscape. Focus is clearly on the visualization of landscape whereby places are cued as meaningful behavioral contexts. The tourist's point of view or, more specifically, the sightseer's point of view provides the general context for my evaluating the visual experiencing of landscape. In no other activity is the visual orienting to landscape as important. My overall objective in presenting this book is to elaborate the language of landscape visualization. It is not my intention to treat landscape as a language in and of itself. My intention is to assess the vocabulary by which landscape as visual display may be conceptualized as scenery. I view my endeavor as a necessary prerequisite to answering the range of questions posed.

Chapter 2

Visualizing Landscape

We are children of our landscape; it dictates behavior and even thought in the measure to which we are responsive to it.

LAWRENCE DURRELL

By the word *landscape* I mean the visible environment that one might see, be it rural or urban. A landscape is a visual world spread spatially before the eyes. It is a container of physical structure and functional meaning in the traditional sense of landscape study. It may also be conceptualized as a visual array in which places, as centers of behavioral intention, are variously cued. As Yi-Fu Tuan writes: "The eyes explore the visual field and abstract from it certain objects, points of focus, perspectives." Thus study of landscape visualization concerns not only the reality of landscape, but also the images derived as repositories of place meaning formed and interpreted in the mind. Behavior, notes geographer Jay Appleton, is influenced by a person's attitude toward the environment, not so much as it is, but as he thinks it is.[1]

An image is a representation of reality. Rudolf Arnheim maintains that images have three primary dimensions: sign, picture, and symbol. These dimensions do not represent kinds of images, but rather describe three functions fulfilled by them. An image serves merely as a sign to the extent that it stands for a particular context without reflecting its characteristics visually. Words on a billboard convey meaning but they themselves do not picture the thing communicated. Images are pictures to the extent that they portray things located at a lower level of abstractness than they are themselves. Pictures in a magazine are only approximate icons of the things portrayed. An image serves as a symbol to the extent that it portrays a thing at a higher level of abstractness than the symbol itself. As simile or metaphor the thing portrayed represents some higher order of meaning beyond itself. Every image performs the task of reasoning, Arnheim writes, by "fusing sensory appearance and generic concepts into one unified cognitive statement."[2]

Images are condensed and abstracted in memory as a store of visual experience. Verbal language is a part of this storing function. Visual images coded verbally may be retrieved verbally. "Yes, it was a beautiful sunset," one might say. Where the experience was vivid, however, words may be accompanied by a visual representation. In the case of the remembered sunset a rethinking of a specific sky's varied colors, or the colors of some generalized generic sunset, may project in the mind's eye. A sunset may be remembered for itself or as it associates in the mind with other meanings. It might signify end-of-day relaxation for example. This essay is concerned with such images, although emphasis will not be given remembered images per se, but the circumstances of vividness that make images memorable. Psychologist E. De Bono has coined an easily remembered definition of memory. "A memory," he writes, "is what is left behind when something happens and does not completely unhappen."[3] I am interested in those conditions, especially of the landscape itself, that discourage the "unhappening" of visual experience.

LANDSCAPE COGNITION

Numerous students of landscape visualization have sought to summarize the mysteries of environmental cognition. To architect Amos Rapoport, people react to landscapes globally and affectively before they analyze them and evaluate them in specific terms. Objects first arouse a feeling that provides an unconscious background for the specific images of consciousness. This background predisposes the viewer to search for specific cues to place meaning. To Rapoport, cues are noticeable differences: visual elements that differ from their context. The architect, in rendering a built environment, can strive to encode cues in design in order to elicit specific place meanings and thus influence behavior. Although it is a person's interpretation of place as social situation that influences behavior, it is the landscape as physical environment that provides the cues to that interpretation. Rapoport emphasizes that place meanings are not constructed *de novo* in each new behavioral circumstance because, once learned, images of place become templates for future action. Therefore, images not only remind, but they also predict and prescribe.[4]

Architect Peter Smith defines cognition as the use of memory to make sense of phenomena and, if necessary, to calculate the requisite motor responses. Borrowing from clinical psychology, he carefully differentiates the function of the limbic brain and that of the neocortex. The primitive or limbic brain controls the visceral functions of the body, the deep-rooted responses concerned with emotions. It is responsible for conscious arousal, although most of its work falls below the threshold of consciousness. The neocortex controls "higher" mental functions such as rational thought as rooted in verbal ability. Smith sees two opposed tendencies. The neocortex promotes order and stability or homeostasis: the tendency to make what is comprehended conform to already internalized patterns. The limbic brain seeks new combinations of patterns, novelty, surprise. It is an incentive to exploration and the uncertainties of exploration. Memory works at both levels. In the first instance it is covert and in the second it is overt.[5]

Scholars have looked primarily at conscious memory. De Bono sees the memory matrix building from childhood. Basic concepts ordering the world are formulated as things in the environment are fit into categories of increasingly sophisticated discrimination. Basic mental schemas become enriched in detail. Rates of information assimilation gradually level off as perception is increasingly monopolized by the familiar. He speculates that for adults perhaps 90 percent of the familiar environment remains "unseen" by the conscious mind. Input slackens as an individual becomes used to a given landscape or kind of landscape. Unconsciously, the limbic brain acts to filter out signals from the environment as it selects input worthy of conscious attention and deliberate thought. As patterns become incised in memory they dominate in the competition for attention. The mind becomes progressively biased in favor of the familiar and the person becomes predisposed to see what experience, stored in memory, suggests ought to be seen.[6]

For purposes of future discussion it might do well to note De Bono's differentiation of environmental "preferences" vis-à-vis the limbic versus the neocortex of the brain. In visual terms, the limbic brain seeks the exoticness of pronounced rhythms, gigantism, and vivid color. The neocortex prefers harmonic relationships between elements and coherence where the whole is much greater than the sum of its parts. De Bono writes:

> The music of Bach is said to stimulate both intellect and emotion. The mathematical relationships of canon and fugue, the overriding sense of serial order and coherent patterns, appeal to the neocortex. When this is directly related to a chorale of measured and profound simplicity and simple rhythm, the result makes a deep impact because here is a dialectic relationship between the complex and intellectual, and the simple and elemental.

So also, he concludes, landscape should cradle as well as stimulate the mind.[7]

Again, borrowing from clinical psychology, Smith also differentiates the neocortex according to left and right functions. The left hemisphere is the seat of rational thought as rooted in verbal skill and mathematical, analytical, and deductive proficiencies. It processes visual input in a serial, logical manner. In landscape terms, the left cerebrum tends to focus on verbal information such as advertising, store names, street signs. The right cerebrum, on the other hand, is the seat of pattern recognition, especially spatial patterns. "It perceives in holistic manner, and thus searches for aspects contributing to unity, coherence, and pattern." Smith considers it the seat of aesthetic sensibility. In landscape terms, the right hemisphere is selective in its vision in favor of such abstractions as shape, location, color, texture, tone, and rhythm.[8]

It is not my purpose to synthesize the literature of sensory perception. Nonetheless, concern here with the basic aspects of cognition cannot but clarify later focus on landscape visualization. It should be kept in mind, however, that the outlines of human cognition have been traced primarily through contrived laboratory studies conducted by physiological psychologists.[9] The extent to which these generalizations apply to the behavioral circumstances of actual landscapes has been little demonstrated. As living organisms people are equipped with sensing organs comprised of highly specialized nerve endings variously clustered to accept energy messages transmitted by the environment. Information is conveyed by electromagnetic, mechanical, and chemical impingements on these sensory receptors with each organ sensitive to only a small part of the total range of possible stimuli. Thus the eyes, for example, are only sensitive to light waves between 390 and 700 millimicrons—a range approximately 1/70 of the total electromagnetic spectrum.[10] Sense organs, particularly those sensitive to light, sound, gravitational pull, and movement, tend to be bilaterally paired. That is, they are located symmetrically on either side of the body. With paired receptors, the cognition of such spatial abstractions as distance, direction, and horizontal-vertical differentiation is facilitated. For example, a person's eyes are set about sixty to seventy millimeters apart and the patterns of stimulation from external objects projected on each retina differ slightly, helping to induce a sense of distance perspective, among other effects.

Traditionally, visual perception has been conceptualized as a rapid succession of still images racing through the mind. As interest in a landscape increases the eyes focus on particular objects and the derived images are made more vivid through conscious thought. Once interest is lost, visual awareness continues only as a low-grade, subconscious scanning of environment. Cognitive input obtains from only a relatively small portion of the visual field as measured on either side of a direct line of focus. The visual field is shaped like an oval that extends approximately 180 degrees horizontally and 150 degrees vertically. It is sharp and clear at the center and increasingly vague toward the periphery; the information gathered peripherally is used primarily to cue focusing.[11] Objects are distinguished according to the patterns of light intensity transmitted from their surfaces. Thus the elemental impressions of the visual world are those of surface and edge.

In dealing with a complex light patterning, the mind attempts to simplify the visual structure by focusing on the most profound transitions or breaks in the perceived surface. These edges make objects stand out from the background or separate one part of an object from another part. Important visual cues include the size of objects relative to one another, their relative location, and the differences in light, shade, and color. The brain reduces events to their simplest qualities and the details of display are then organized as simplistic super-structures. The simplified picture becomes a predictive device with which the eyes continue to search for visual meaning. People seek a sense of rightness or correctness in the visual environment predicated on past experience. Indeed, a visual image may be construed as much on what an individual thinks he is going to see as on what is actually there to be seen.

In seeing, complex visual fields are reduced to sets of basic interrelationship. For example, the mind searches for economic spatial unity in the ordering of optical differences. Proximity is, perhaps, the simplest condition for establishing a sense of visual wholeness. Thus objects that are close together are grouped together. Elements are also unified on the basis of similarity or equality. Equal sizes or similar shapes, directions, corresponding colors, and textures all produce a dynamic tendency to be seen together. The sense of continuance is another factor. Every linear unit has kinetic inertia because it tends to be continued directionally with the movement of the eye. A straight line tends to be seen continuing as a straight line, a wavy line with the repetition of its original rhythm. The mind also searches for closure in order to find forms with a sense of stable unity. Closure gives a sense of boundedness. The mind also searches for opposites. The brain picks opposite pairs among the segments of visual reality, although the sense of opposition is usually mediated by a sense of center in order to reconcile bipolar tendencies. Thus planner Kevin Lynch writes: "Physical characteristics, to the extent that they are over the threshold of attention at all, seem to radiate their image conceptually to some degree, spreading out from a center."[12]

Within the nervous system energy is transduced into elec-trical events in response to changing environmental stimulation. Such change may derive from a change in the positioning or character of the various sensing organs. Our eyes, for example, are constructed to provide constantly changing views that serve to enhance awareness. The eyes are in a continual state of oscillation or tremor, each eye being suspended between three pairs of muscles for this purpose. Awareness also results from actual change in the environment, including a change in body position relative to the environment. As a stimulus increases in intensity a point is reached beyond which awareness or acuity begins. This point varies from circumstance to circumstance and from one kind of behavior to another.

Below the stimulus threshold, perceptual input fails to excite awareness. If this happens over a lengthy period, there develops a tendency for the sensing system to become habituated or insensitive to changes when they do occur. This deadening effect, or sensory adaptation, occurs whenever constant stimulus "washes out" sensations. Perceptual constancy may result from an ambiguous landscape where the messages from the environment are obscured or unclear. Both excessively simple and excessively complex landscapes invite loss of acuity. The former provide relatively little stimulus and become boring, while the latter, by nature of their overwhelming stimulus value, force the brain to oversimplify or strip away information with accompanying degrees of stress. Ideally, landscape will neither bore nor stress, but, rather, will contain only sufficient complexity to excite and interest.

Complexity in landscape is a function of violated expectations. Environmental complexity exists when noticeable differences are recognized in the face of more simplistic anticipations. When these differences overwhelm the expected, the mind becomes confused and must seek different memory patterns to interpret the scene. Landscapes that hold viewer interest are those that build up viewer expectations, but then also noticeably depart from them. Architects Rapoport and Ron Hawkes advise creation of complexity in the landscape through the careful manipulation of form. As people pass through a landscape their senses should be continually treated to the unexpected in order to sharpen awareness. However, variety should not deviate too far from expectations, or frustration and confusion will result. "Building up expectations and then noticeably departing from them is the principle behind the creation of complexity through the manipulation of variety."[13]

Figures 2.1 and 2.2
Distorting space with a telephoto
lens—Gold Beach, Oregon. The
sense of spatial relationship
between things is enhanced when
a scene is "telescoped" by a
telephoto lens. Through such
distortion spatial awareness, the
sense of distance between things,
is amplified. Expectations are
violated, calling attention to what
normally is taken for granted.
Imminent contact is implied.

SPATIAL LEARNING

Once the position of an object has been identified within its
environmental context, it is said to be related spatially (in both
the two-dimensional and three-dimensional sense) to other
objects. The memory develops a cognitive schema or "cognitive map" to enable spatial prediction. People are rarely aware
of moving or otherwise functioning in space. But when the
positioning of things appears distorted, as when binoculars or
a telephoto lens optically compresses distance, space does
become an overt thing. Two photographs shot along an
Oregon coast leave two distinct impressions (figs. 2.1 and 2.2).
The first approximates normal vision. The two rocks intercept
the incoming waves and the expanse of sand suggests a broad

Figure 2.3

Crowdedness—Art fair at Springfield, Illinois. Space looms important when in short supply. The crowding of persons and things amplifies spatial relationship by literally bringing things into physical contact.

open beach. But in the second photograph distance has been contracted. The rocks loom out of water which seems to boil as some kind of primordial sea. What seems commonplace becomes extraordinary when one's sense of spatial appropriateness is violated. Lack of space, as when things crowd in upon an individual to deny (or potentially deny) freedom of action, also brings the space concept to the fore. With claustrophobia, space does not appear telescoped; it is simply felt inadequate to the needs at hand (fig. 2.3). Lack of space may require constant evasive action to avoid unwanted physical contact. Thus the search for space can become a constant social preoccupation.

Psychologist Jean Piaget hypothesizes that children develop through four stages of spatial awareness: the sensorimotor, preoperational, concrete operational, and formal operational periods.[14] In the first stage (from birth to about two years) children begin to construct a system of relationships between objects based on the manipulation of objects. The infant associates self-initiated action and related body sensations as isolated events and, with the coordination of sight and movement, the infant learns to relate objects perceived at different times. Psychologist Robert Beck writes of the child's growing awareness of direction, distance, and vertical dimension.

> At first the baby is placed on his stomach (facing down), then on his back (facing up). In the crawling stage, the infant lives in the horizontal plane—his line of sight and mode of exploration is highly uniplanar, action occurs toward and away from objects at

his own level of height. Later the child raises his head and eventually stands up; he enters the space of the vertical plane— up and down become coordinated, right and left gain more freedom. As the child structures space and forms object relations, innumerable spatial connotations develop. About the same time the acquisition of binocular vision expands the two-dimensional into the three-dimensional world. The distinctions of symmetrical from non-symmetrical relations come later still.[15]

In Piaget's second period of spatial maturity (roughly from two to seven years) the child is able to transform the mental construct of his surroundings in very elementary ways. Although he is able to realize that one arrives at different locations when one goes in different directions, he is still unable to conceptualize the reverse sequence of locations along a given route. The third stage (roughly from seven to eleven years) is marked by increased sophistication of image transformation. For example, what takes place in one direction can also take place in the opposite direction. The child can look at objects in space from a multiple of viewpoints and can express these experiences using abstract language. By the end of this period the child has grasped the following spatial concepts: (1) proximity, the nearness of objects one to another; (2) separation, the disassociation of objects; (3) order, the spatial succession of objects; (4) enclosure, the surrounding of objects by other objects; and (5) continuity, the totality of objects seen as a complete distribution in space.[16]

In Piaget's last period of spatial maturity (roughly eleven years and older) the child is liberated from concrete reality in that he is able to pose truly abstract hypotheses. He can use spatial images that entail unreal transformations from apparent reality. Topological transformations involve rules of proximity, separation, sequence, and closure, which remain invariant under continuous deformation. Projective transformations involve spatial relations constructed according to various points of view as when the surface of a sphere is reproduced on a flat surface in different ways. Geometrical transformations involve metrical relationships that coordinate space with respect to a system of outside reference points. Most people use a Euclidean geometry to order events in a plane or two-dimensional space.[17]

Each individual develops his own style of organizing space cognitively according to his own particular history of space learning. Once an individual discovers a successful mental response to a particular kind of spatial problem, he then tends to develop it as a distinctive cognitive pattern, a template upon which to organize the world as visual array. An individual forms an impression or tentative picture of the landscape on the basis of earlier experience and focuses attention on objects that fit well within these expectations. Initial conceptualization influences later conceptualization by providing a framework into which later information is placed.

PLACE LEARNING

As centers of behavioral intention, places nest in space variously defined at different scales of comprehension. Landscapes as visual arrays not only have spatial dimension, they also contain place meanings cued in part by cognized spatial form or format. Children not only develop sophisticated spatial capabilities, they also develop sophisticated place orientations. They mature into worlds of increasingly complex place relationships. It seems a reasonable assumption that this maturation also progresses by stages. For discussion purposes, I hypothesize five periods of increasing place awareness: the self-focused period (from birth to about three months), the parent-focused period (probably from three months to about one year), the period of bounded home range (from about one year to three years), the period of expanded home range (from about three years to ten years), and the period of fully integrated activity space (roughly from ten years).[18]

To the newborn infant, life is a blur of sensation: a sea of sight, sound, smell, and feeling. By remembering highly repetitive stimulus patterns, he slowly comes to recognize certain states of existence. Most important, he separates himself from his surroundings as an entity or object of the most profound place significance. Essentially immobile, the infant's self-generated activities are body focused in an initial stage of place awareness. In the second stage, an infant's parents (and especially his mother) become an equal focus of value. Tuan writes: "Mother may well be the first enduring and independent object in the infant's world of fleeting impressions. Later she is recognized by the child as his essential shelter and dependable source of physical and psychological comfort."[19] An emerging sense of place appropriateness is tied to a parent's availability or accessibility.

As the infant learns to crawl and thus propel himself in a horizontal plane, objects apart from him and his parents take on meaning through use. As Beck notes, the concrete primitive meaning of physical exploration is supplemented and elaborated by use and function of objects. Once a child learns to walk, his world of valuable objects potentially expands exponentially, although most children's movements are highly contained within localized home territories. Thus the third stage of place awareness involves a bounded home range where the child becomes attached not only to significant persons and other significant objects, but also to localities of interest seen to variously contain persons, objects, and ongoing activities. To a young child, Tuan notes, a place is a large and somewhat immobile type of object which represents a locus of some recognized satisfaction or dissatisfaction. At first such a large thing has less meaning than small things because, unlike portable toys or security blankets, they cannot be handled and moved easily.[20] Nonetheless, the child does come to value places as things to be occupied bodily rather than possessed merely through handling. At this stage the child becomes concerned to name places and to develop a sense of territoriality or possession relative to close-by places or to places used frequently or intimately. He begins to learn to play the roles appropriate to different kinds of places.

In the fourth stage the child's bounded home range is expanded by disjointed route/destination combinations. As a regular passenger in the family automobile he develops a clear sense of "here" and "there," but he seldom has a complete notion of the intervening linkages between such places. Again, Tuan writes: "Adults have acquired the habit of taking mental note of where things are and how to go from one place to another. Children, on the other hand, are caught up in the excitement of people, things, and events; going from one place to another is not their responsibility." The child's geographic horizon expands but not necessarily step by step toward the larger scale. The child's interest and knowledge may focus first on the small local community, and then on the city, skipping the neighborhood; and from the city his interest may jump to the nation and foreign places, skipping the region.[21] In this process, an ability develops to categorize settings according to generic "place-types." The rural countryside is seen to differ from the small town which, in turn, is seen to differ from the big city. His recognition that different kinds of behavior are often appropriate in these varied places grows in sophistication.

In the fifth stage of place awareness the child has learned to function effectively in a fully integrated activity space. He, himself, remains the viewpoint from which the world is contemplated. His parents remain a primary focus for support, although he has escaped, in large measure, the confines of home as a bounded space. His effective world stretches beyond home to school and recreational places. The meaningful behavior settings of his world are effectively related across differences of scale. He knows how different settings are linked and he can negotiate effectively between them. In addition, he has developed his own style of being in places differently defined. He has learned the behaviors appropriate to the different kinds of places important in his world, to the different places necessary to his own satisfaction in life. He has a sophisticated sense of how different place meanings are cued. He recognizes sophisticated nuances of place meaning as they are encoded in landscape. He carries a sophisticated cognitive map of the world comprised of linked sets of place expectations.[22]

PLACE VERSUS SPACE

Whereas spatial learning has more to do with conceptualizing the positioning of objects defined as places, place learning has more to do with conceptualizing the content of localities so objectified. Place learning goes well beyond the mere spatial dimension to embrace the full spectrum of meaning by which places are anticipated and used (fig. 2.4). Nonetheless, much confusion exists in geography and other disciplines as to the relationship between these two concepts. Many scholars use the two terms synonymously. For example, a concept such as *sense of place* is made to stand as a convenient alternative for the concept *spatial sense*. For many geographers, the place concept is firmly rooted in notions of location variously expressed.

Figure 2.4

New office and shopping complex—New Orleans. A new "place" has been created, its meaning clearly outlined in the sign announcing its creation. The sign is intended to heighten expectation regarding future use, to predispose people in prescribed ways.

Geographer Donald Meinig writes: "Place commonly refers to a definite area, a fixed location." Again, for Edward Relph location is only incidental, with space providing a mere context for place.[23]

Tuan links place and space, defining the two as complementary ideas. He writes: "In experience the meaning of space often merges with that of place." He continues: "From security of place we are aware of the openness, freedom, and threat of space, and vice versa. Furthermore, if we think of space as that which allows movement, then place is pause; each pause in movement makes it possible for location to be transformed into place." For Tuan space is given by the ability to move. Movements are directed toward, or repulsed by places as objects. Space can be variously experienced as the relative location of places, as the distances that separate or link places,

Figure 2.5

Enclosed space—Houston's Galleria. To architects "space" is a three-dimensional enclosure as opposed to the two-dimensional configuration geographers conceptualize. Architectural space is designed to enclose or encompass. Such space also can be partially filled to excite the eye.

and, more abstractly, as the area defined by a network of places. Much of this argument appears based on a concern for landscape visualization, and the symbolizations based on that visualization. His definitions of space and place appear to derive from a felt need to define relationships that can be seen in landscape. The idea of space he equates with wide-open vistas or panoramas implying unhindered movement. The idea of place he equates with enclosure. "Enclosed and humanized space is place," he writes. "Compared to space, place is a calm center of established values," he continues. Thus place is shelter and space is venture, the former attachment and the latter freedom. The "boundedness of place" is seen to contrast with the "exposure of space."[24]

Unlike geographers, architects see space in three rather than two dimensions. Space is something that gives form to place as one aspect of place meaning. Enclosure defines space as a kind of volume as implicit in the photograph of Houston's Galleria Shopping Center (fig. 2.5). A giant mobile hangs from the ceiling to enliven visually and give character to this open expanse. For the architect, space does not merely locate in a geographical sense. Rather, it surrounds, or potentially surrounds, in an all-encompassing sense. Christian Norberg-Schultz writes: "Whereas 'space' denotes the three-dimensional organization of the elements which make up a place, 'character' denotes the general 'atmosphere' which is the most comprehensive property of any place." Places, he notes, are designated by nouns as they are considered "real things that exist." Space, as a system of relations, is denoted instead by prepositions. He writes: "In our daily life we hardly talk about 'space,' but about things that are 'over' or 'under,' 'before' or 'behind' each other, or we use prepositions such as 'at,' 'in,' 'within,' 'on,' 'upon,' 'to,' 'from,' 'along,' 'next.' " Prepositions denote topological relations that represent the abstract essence of space. The other characteristics of place are denoted by adjectives. Space, he concludes, is a problem of orientation and place a problem of expectation. "When man dwells, he is simultaneously located in space and exposed to a certain environmental character. The two psychological functions involved may be called 'orientation' and 'identification.' To gain an existential foothold, man has to be able to *orientate* himself; he has to know where he is. But he also has to *identify* himself with the environment, that is, he has to know *how* he is a certain place."[25]

It is in this latter sense of place as identification that landscape visualization moves beyond the realm of spatial preoccupation. A place is an object or entity conceptualized in two-dimensional geographical space and it has three-dimensional spatial form, but, above all, it is a focus of meaning, character, identity. It is in the recognition of this identity, even when such recognition is totally devoid of "spatial" implication, that the concept of place has real value. This is a recognition that Tuan emphasizes. "Places are centers of value," he writes. "They attract or repel in finely shaded degrees. To attend them even momentarily is to acknowledge their reality and value."[26]

In visual terms, space is the background for objects. What makes a city skyline impressive is not so much the bulk of the

Figure 2.6

Space as background—San Francisco. Space is background, being less tangible than the thing it is seen to contain. Space surrounds. Here the TransAmerica Tower makes a powerful architectural statement silhouetted against a background of fog-shrouded sky.

buildings grouped, but the openness of the sky against which they silhouette. San Francisco's TransAmerica Tower communicates as the perfect corporate logo (if not city logo) given its striking profile viewed against an open spatial background (fig. 2.6). Space is less tangible than the objects it contains. It is the "ground" for the "figure." Space is what remains between objects, because space is derived from its material boundaries. At Albany's Empire State Center, effective use of space, the sense of separation communicated both in sky and water, creates profound visual excitement (fig. 2.7). But it is objects and not spaces that usually attract attention. Architect Robert Yudell notes: "It is not surprising that forms are more often the focus of our attention than space or movement in space. Space is typically thought of as a void or as the absence of solid, and movement thought of as a domain separate from its existence

Figure 2.7

Space as separation—Empire State Center, Albany, New York. Space is separation. It is that which remains between objects. Here, buildings relate across spaces variously defined by sky and sky reflected by water.

in space."[27] Space stands as a useful concept to be imposed on the world to help make experience coherent. Space by itself, however, is an insufficient schemata to comprehend how people structure and use landscapes. Rather, it is the concept of place, a schemata of focused meaning cued in part by spatial form, that deserves attention.

Place is the sum of all objects that combine to give a sense of behavioral focus through expectation. Places have identity or character through the satisfactions or dissatisfactions anticipated as variously cued by objects both animate and inanimate. Identity, landscape critic Ian Nairn writes, is a "unique configuration" of all the objects that go to make up a place. Implicit in these objects are behavioral expectations. Accordingly, the role of the architect is to recognize and exploit the identities of place in such a manner as to match the human needs implicit. This matching, Nairn emphasizes, is a problem of recognizing identities and of giving them visual limits, of identifying their limits with visual articulation. The way to an expressive and exciting landscape, he concludes, is through the creation of separate identities, each framing an essential part of the whole. One creates these identities through the physical relationships of objects as they form spatial sequences. He writes: "The difference between sequences in different places is a very large part of identity."[28] Concern with the spatial dimension in landscape study, therefore, might be limited, following Nairn's argument, to the sequential relationships between the objects which differentiate places.

SCENERY AS PLACE

Visualization is built up from images that occur successively in time. It is a search for figure and ground relationship whereby sharp edges define objects against their backgrounds. It is also a search for meaningful object groupings based on principles of proximity, similarity, continuance, closure, opposition, and centrality. Places are categories whereby objects are seen to be grouped in a shared space. As places are used, satisfactions and even dissatisfactions accrue, laying the basis for anticipated behavior in the future. Thus the objects of place come to symbolize through association place satisfactions and dissatis-factions previously experienced. They stand as cues to place meaning whereby future behavior is directed. Conscious land-scape visualization involves two steps in a sequence of visual exploration. The first phase might be thought of as "space-covering," and the second as "place-organizing."

Space-covering search is a systematic scanning of landscape for meaningful cues to place. It may frequently dissolve into covert rather than overt activity little above the threshold of awareness. It is a search for cues to place meaning deemed sig-nificant given behavioral predispositions. Place-organizing search is a more specific visual probing of landscape toward the uncovering of expected patterns that validate cues already found. It is essentially a problem-solving behavior: a con-frontation with unanswered questions, a deliberate posing of alternative answers, a choosing of specific alternatives of action usually with some degree of efficiency. As a focusing and structuring of attention, it probably reflects more the influence of the neocortex than that of the limbic brain, and the right hemisphere rather than the left. Place-organizing search decodes the landscape to predict and direct behavior. To that extent it is an ordering of reality in terms of selected landscape images.[29]

People learn to play roles appropriate to landscape. People learn to behave effectively in specific places according to be-haviors ongoing. They learn the social rules appropriate to places as behavior settings. They probably also tend to seek the

---

kinds of places experienced in the past as most rewarding, comfortable, secure. Each individual "sees" a landscape and its place implications differently. However, as place meanings represent symbolic interaction rooted in social reality, people tend to share similar place predispositions to varying degrees. Nairn writes: "While every individual may assign self-consciously or unself-consciously an identity to particular places, these identities are nevertheless combined intersubjectively to form a common identity. Perhaps this occurs because we experience more or less the same objects and activities and because we have been taught to look for certain qualities of place emphasized by our cultural group."[30]

Some places are overtly public and elicit widely stereotyped behaviors. Meanings are carefully coded through design. Cues are made, through redundancy, to add up to amplified, clearly legible statements of place. Qualities of "placeness" draw attention to themselves, declaring themselves overtly. Places are thereby made to stand out in their surroundings. Because of their centrality or clarity of form, remarkable size, exceptional architecture, or unusual natural features they possess high imageability.[31] Other places are more private in that their meanings are more personal. Such places tend not to be exaggerated in form, or overt in cue. Their meanings are subtle. No one set of cues, nor one structural format, communicates implicit place ideas. Place meanings are attached by various people in various ways. The affective bonds between people and such places are highly personalized.

The quest for scenery is a particular kind of space-covering and place-organizing activity which involves distinctive role playing. It is a quest for public and private place identities characterized by visual delight. The sightseer, as tourist, quests visual interest as satisfying entertainment. Because the sightseer's orientation to landscape is essentially aesthetic, concern focuses on the manner by which objects of place combine in stimulating ways, especially in sequential relationships. The sightseer's role is what Appleton calls the "spontaneous enjoyment of landscape." Tourists also function as outsiders. They do not seek to fully penetrate places as behavior settings, but, rather, are content to move about the peripheries of ongoing activity. Their participation with natives is vicarious. Tuan writes that tourists judge places "by appearance" or by "some formal canon of beauty" and that special effort is required "to empathize with the lives and values of the inhabitants."[32]

The sightseer's orientation to place lies across that spectrum of place intention characterized by Relph as "behavioral insideness" and "empathetic insideness." The former consists of being in a place and seeing it as a set of objects having distinctive observable qualities. It is a deliberate attending to the appearances of place. Relph writes: "Patterns, structures and content . . . tell us we are *here* rather than somewhere else. These patterns are, in the first instance, those of our immediate experience, and perhaps the most important element of this is sight." The sightseer, in other words, is first a collector of place cues. Such comprehension, according to Relph, requires charting the relationships between objects thus to illustrate the various modes of relationship. "Empathetic insideness," on the other hand, adds a deliberate effort at place identity. It is a willingness to be open to the significances of a place, to know and respect its symbols. Relph emphasizes: "To be inside a place empathetically is to understand that place as rich in meaning, and hence to identify with it, for these meanings are not only linked to the experiences and symbols of those whose place it is, but also stem from one's own experience." In this way sightseers do not merely look at a place, but seek to appreciate the essential elements of its identity within the context of their own memories.[33]

Sightseers process the visual imagery of landscape in search of memorable views. They scan the physical form of landscape responsive to cues of visual delight. Thus a place of visual interest is defined whenever the scanning eye pauses in its survey. Mental pictures are composed as attention shifts from cue to cue, the mind seeking to establish place meaning in terms of worthwhile pictures. Place as picture is the primary objective. Only occasionally do sightseers consciously insert themselves as potential actors into the ongoing action of a scene. Scenes exist primarily to be remembered or forgotten as visual arrays of the moment both stimulating and comforting to the psyche.

The search for scenery is, in part, a learned behavior. Each society has its codes for playing the sightseer's role which individual tourists may or may not master well. Members of a society share various ways of looking at landscape or of composing scenes. They learn rigidly conditioned points of view. For example, the graphic arts, especially photography, have instilled set preferences for composing mental pictures. Indeed, John Ewart even uses the camera through analogy to describe visualization. He writes: "It may be that we all 'compose' as we look at a scene of any kind, though the degree of subtlety with which we do this will vary from person to person. Our field of vision is a limited one, and we move it about like a view-finder of a camera, and the very act of selecting a point at which to gaze or 'take-in' the view presupposes that, at such a point, the several features we have been admiring separately all come together in a happy mixture."[34]

The search for scenery is to some degree physiologically driven. Human perception is selective rather than inclusive. Although the retinal mosaic contains innumerable details, attention is paid only to some of them. Parts of the mosaic that stand out from their surroundings through contrasting color, size, intensity, or movement, or through novelty, draw involuntary attention. Attention-drawing characteristics are, undoubtedly, part of our biological inheritance from when man played the role of hunter in a hostile environment. Appleton has explored this notion. For man the hunter, seeing without being seen was the essence of life. He required both "prospect," the unimpeded opportunity to see, and "refuge," the opportunity to hide. Modern man, according to Appleton, has inherited these visual needs and, although he no longer needs them for survival, he incorporates them into landscape visualization, especially the quest for scenery. Appleton writes: "The removal of urgent necessity does not put an end to the machinery which evolved to cope with . . . [the environment]; rather it frees that machinery to achieve different objectives which themselves are constantly changing with the aspirations and caprices of society. What was a functional disposition of environmental objects becomes conventionalized into a type or series of types which we regard as harmonious because they continue to give us satisfaction." Such thinking echoes psychologist Carl Jung's notion of "archetypal images" which "live on as systems of reaction and disposition" to determine life in an "invisible manner" below the level of conscious memory.[35]

For the sightseer, scenery is something that comes readily to mind. Much that people see requires effort or what Stephen Kaplan calls "voluntary attention."[36] "When one is tempted by distractions, but pays attention, as it were, by an effort of the will, that attention is voluntary." By contrast, some attention occurs "in spite of ourselves." "It requires no effort and is fully involuntary." Certain kinds of patterns or events prove innately fascinating and not only attract but hold the eye. These landscapes, as scenic places, easily involve the viewer. They display some complexity, but an overall coherence is also readily discernible. These are the places that satisfy as visual displays. Involuntary attention is a cultural manifestation embedded in a society's propensity to value certain kinds of visual display as scenic. Involuntary attention also derives from human biological inheritance that predisposes focus.

The visualization of landscape as scenery is a diverse topic which may be approached from innumerable points of view. It is a concern with the images of landscape as rooted in basic cognition. It is a concern for the spatial dimensions of reality learned in the context of moving in two- and three-dimensional spheres of reference. It is a concern for places as centers of learned behavioral expectation. Above all, it is a concern for place as scenery and thus it involves sightseeing as role playing. In future chapters, therefore, I will be primarily concerned with landscape images of heightened visual delight, the images of scenic view sought by sightseers. I will begin in the next chapter by answering: What are the basic visual components of landscape? How do they combine as scenic views?

Chapter 3

Landscape
as
Prospect
and
Refuge

What is it that we like about
landscape, and why do we
like it?

JAY APPLETON

In landscape, the sightseer seeks views that compose involuntarily in the mind's eye as satisfying place images. Sightseeing
is a search for scenes by which the objects of place can be
effectively discovered and related. A view, as a complex of
objects (a kind of place in itself), can be categorized according
to basic components. These components include: (1) extent of
view or the distance over which sight is effective; (2) fore-
ground-middleground-background discontinuities or the
existence of multiple horizons; (3) enframement by which
sight is bounded; (4) focal points that serve as attention getters;
and (5) sense of security implicit in focal points that imply
refuge.[1] Effective views contain prospects that enable viewers
to survey considerable distances over several successive
horizons. "Panoramas," for example, are grand uninterrupted
prospects which sweep to far horizons across all or nearly all of
one's field of vision (fig. 3.1). "Vistas," a more common kind
of prospect, are views conspicuously bounded or enframed

Figure 3.1

Panorama—highway near
Tribune, Kansas. Here the land is
flat, stretching to a distant
horizon, and the motorist is
drawn inextricably to the
common vanishing point of
highway, railroad, and power
line. The world is a panorama.
The viewer is left with a sense of
the infinite, the panorama
stretching both forward and
laterally, seemingly endlessly.
Here also is a classic prospect in
the perspectivist's tradition.

(fig. 3.2). Both panoramas and vistas may be anchored visually
by focal points that, as they attract attention, draw the eye.
Effective views also offer refuge, a feeling of security in the
suggestion of protection. I deal first with the sense of prospect
and then turn to security or refuge.

PROSPECT

The sense of distance is limited by our vision in that we cannot
see an object that is farther from us than about 3,500 times its
size. We categorize space according to the functional effectiveness of different distances. Architect Paul Spreiregen notes that
a person who stands three to ten feet from us is in "close" relationship, eight feet being normal conversation distance. In this
range we can speak in normal voice and catch the subtleties of
speech and facial gesture which constitute conversation. We
can distinguish facial expression up to about forty feet, recognize a friend's face up to about eighty feet, and discern body
gesture to about 450 feet. Finally, we can see people up to 4,000
feet, beyond which they are too small to be seen at all.[2] Long
distances are cued by estimating the sizes of known objects
including people. The same object seen at different distances is
depicted on the retina by images of different sizes subtending
different visual angles. Individuals maintain a constancy
regarding object size and shape even though the size and shape
of retinal projections vary. Perceived changes are concep-

Figure 3.2
Vista—Edinburgh, Scotland.
Climb the Scott Monument and
this is what you see. All the
elements of an attractive view are
here. The eye is carried easily to
the far horizon where the Firth of
Forth serves as background. The
street below provides the
foreground, the wooded suburbs
the middleground. The principal
focal point is located at the end of
the street where foreground and
middleground meet. The flag to
the left and the monument to the
right suggest enframement, as
does the street below.

tualized as distance differentials rather than as changes in the
objects themselves.[3]

Artists during the Renaissance developed techniques for
replicating graphically the linear perspective of distance so
visualized, what James Gibson calls "artificial perspective." In
our modern era of widespread graphic communication, most
people learn to see in those terms. Even where two lines do not
converge at a vanishing point on some far horizon, we, nonetheless, conceptualize depth of view in landscape in the
"perspectivist manner." Gibson is correct in asserting,
however, that "natural perspective" is quite different from the
artistic device. It derives from the seeing of objects against their
backgrounds. Tadahiko Higuchi echoes this view. "It is not
the object we are looking at that gives us a visual sense of space,
but the object's background." Imagined longitudinal planes
parallel to the line of vision are perceived as having a textural
density. Specifically, a gradual rise in the density of the texture
is perceived as the distance from the viewer increases. Thus in
a line of railroad boxcars stretching toward the horizon as
depicted in figure 3.1, the size of each car seems to decrease
toward the vanishing point.[4]

The shrinking of an object with distance implies a time
dimension, or length of time needed to reach the object.
Although the Edinburgh street shown in figure 3.2 is fixed and
immobile, we tend to read it in action terms. As the eye

Figure 3.3

Terminated vista—Wall Street. What American does not recognize this scene? This view has come to symbolize New York's financial district and, as such, serves as a principal icon of the city. Trinity Church terminates the canyon. The abrupt end of prospect so sharply enframed creates a highly memorable sense of place.

"moves" and "extends," reaching out toward the horizon, so too the road seems to move and extend out toward the horizon. The distortion of perspective carries from one building to the next within a linear pattern of buildings lining such a street. The gradual shrinking of the surfaces actually tends to link the buildings together, and a directional quality is produced. The eye is carried into the view from one focal point to another, the prominent focal points defining intervening horizons or grounds of interest increasingly recessive into the visual field. Enframement increases the intensity of thrust by which the eye penetrates space as vista. Framing focuses attention forward across the sequences of focal points toward the ultimate horizon. The full potential of prospect is achieved when mind encourages body to follow the eye into the view. Prospect, as Jay Appleton argues, gives a sense of movement and, thereby, a sense of freedom.[5]

Figure 3.4

Deflected vista—Birmingham, England. Channeled down the street between the walls of parallel facades, the eye is attracted by and then deflected past the tower, exciting curiosity about what lies ahead still unseen. The motorist is drawn not to an obvious vanishing point, but by a point of mystery beyond which the landscape stands as yet unrevealed. The sense of mystery demands a secondary vista: another chance to explore beyond.

Vistas

Scenes vary in their attractiveness according to the visual relationships struck by various landscape components. For example, distance, multiple horizon, enframement, and focal point combine variously to define different kinds of vistas. I will briefly identify the principal sorts of vistas, using photographs to illustrate. A view along a "terminated vista," or what Gordon Cullen calls a "closed vista," is closed off in the middleground, the object that limits the view serving as an obvious focal point.[6] The view along New York City's Wall Street toward Trinity Church is a classic case (fig. 3.3). Such a vista appears complete, the terminating focus the essence of closure or completion. Stability pervades an implied reaching of an ultimate goal. "Deflected vistas" are similar in structure except that the view is incomplete and instability pervades. The focal point deflects the view at an angle encouraging the mind to yet another unseen secondary vista as the photograph of Birmingham depicts (fig. 3.4).[7] The focal point, whether it is a curve in a street or a building askew at the end of a street, suggests not a termination to visual exploration, but a continuation. The view is bounced toward the unseen, thus heightening anticipation. Implicit is a sense of mystery as to what lies beyond. Undulation is a closely related concept. Undulation occurs as a series of deflected vistas. When one moves along a meandering street a rhythm is set up with views

Figure 3.5

Undulation—Stirling, Scotland.
A series of deflected vistas
produces a sense of undulation.
Here the rhythm of the
meandering street bounces the
eye forward toward the unseen to
create anticipation. The mind
extrapolates the serpentine
pattern forward to set
expectations as to what lies ahead,
an iteration to the right
suggesting an iteration to the left.

shifting sequentially, left and right as the photograph of
Sterling, Scotland, shows (fig. 3.5).[8]

Some vistas appear to retard vision, others to enhance it. A
"screened vista" partially obscures a distant focal point.[9]
Foliage overhanging a street, for example, may make objects
beyond appear even more remote than they actually are. The
pedestrian strains to see the details of a building in downtown
Hartford partially obscured by foliage (fig. 3.6). Masking a
focal point temporarily adds to the excitement of movement,
especially if the goal when revealed in full shows a new face or
a new intensity. A "truncated vista" brings foreground and
background into dramatic juxtaposition as middleground is
hidden from view.[10] As at Cornwall's Land's End, an illusion
makes near distance and far distance appear in the same plane as
directly connected (fig. 3.7). Only with movement, the
topping of the intermediate rise in the road for example, is the
entire space brought together. A "horizontal vista" is constricted by bounding margins in the horizontal as well as the
vertical plane.[11] The motorist's view is constrained along the
horizontal dimension in the motorway interchange pictured
(fig. 3.8). All vistas are laterally bounded by vertical objects
standing in a horizontal plane, but horizontal vistas are
bounded above as well as below and laterally. A related vista,
the "peephole," is severely constricted in this regard. Views
totally enframed by windows or arches serve as examples
(fig. 3.9).[12] In contrast, an "expanding vista" gives a sense of

broadened perspective as when a distant hillside is revealed, widening the prospect from a restricted vista into a suggestion of panorama (fig. 3.10).[13]

Each kind of vista makes a very different visual impact. The physical components that comprise the landscape, both the solid structures (buildings, trees, etc.) and the open spaces (streets, plazas, etc.) have visual impact according to spatial relationships defined here by category of vista. The landscape as seen is not just the sum of its parts, but of its parts summed in distinctive spatial configurations. I have described here some of the set patterns of visual attractiveness that make for highly imageable places. In part, legible landscapes are those within which vistas readily compose themselves to the eye.

The Street as Vista

Landscapes are known primarily from the routes or paths along which people move. Especially in urban places vistas at

Figure 3.7

Truncated vista—Land's End in Cornwall. The eye is carried steadily forward until the highway drops from view. As the eye searches the horizon for visual continuance, the intervening middleground is literally overlooked, the foreground and background appearing to connect directly. The sense of mystery is diminished for the ultimate goal in movement is visible. That which is unknown has simply dropped from view.

Figure 3.8

Horizontal vista—Birmingham, England. A glance from beneath this bridge abutment gives the motorist a view framed in the horizontal as well as the vertical plane. The emphasis is horizontal, as a series of glances follows easily the horizon line. The eye is substantially confined in its landscape survey.

ground level are restricted largely to streets. In cities, buildings rarely stand alone, but are parts of rows viewed with much angular distortion as one passes. Few city buildings exhibit three-dimensionality; rather, they fit together as two-dimensional walls experienced as the sides of urban canyons. These walls provide the vertical bounds by which most vistas are laterally contained. People orient themselves to streets as

Figure 3.9

Peephole vista—East Looe, Cornwall. The harbor is only glimpsed through a portal. The vista is totally confined both vertically and horizontally. Distant vision is profoundly restricted. The eye is drawn forward and held.

Figure 3.10

Expanding vista—Bath, England. What would otherwise be a view of limited scope expands into a panorama on the sweep of hillside in the background. The view is given both depth and vertical dimension by the disclosed slope. The city looms up and away to fully expose itself to view. The eye is liberated.

open spaces, eyes directing courses of action through the open channels. Such may be the dominant feature of the urban sightseer's spatial experience. With increased speed (travel by automobile as opposed to travel on foot, for example), the sense of spatial penetration is enhanced with attention more clearly focused on the street as a linear place of distinctive form. The pedestrian's field of view normally has a 180 degree angle of peripheral vision horizontally and a 150 degree angle vertically, with a clear field of vision 27 degrees high and 45 degrees wide. Of course, these angles decrease as speed increases giving a sense of forward emphasis.[14]

The effectiveness of street as vista is, in part, a function of

Figure 3.11

Street as vista—Nantucket, Massachusetts. Here is displayed the proportions of successful enclosure: the walls of the buildings equal the width of the street in height. In addition, the church serves as an obvious focal point to entice the eye forward, the street both directing and containing the view. People's attraction to such "historical" places as Nantucket is not only a function of old architecture per se, but of buildings and open spaces relating harmoniously as visual configurations.

building height and street width. Landscape architect Barrie Greenbie maintains that outdoor space is most clearly perceived as being pleasantly enclosed when the relationship of the vertical and horizontal dimensions is 4 to 1. The "walls," as in the Nantucket, Massachusetts, street pictured in figure 3.11, must be at least one-quarter the width of the "floor space" and no more than twice the width in height. Architect Yoshinobu Ashihara echoes this view. When the distance/height ratio falls below 1, space grows increasingly intimate, until eventually it is simply cramped. When distance/height equals 1 a balance is achieved, although ratios of 1, 2, or 3 are, according to Ashihara, more satisfying. Rudolf Arnheim reminds us that "the shorter the distance from an object, the greater the visual angle which determines the size of an image received by the eyes. In a constricted environment a relatively small part of a building or space between buildings fills a large area of the visual field and may be surveyable only if the eyes and the head rove back and forth in scanning motions." The more effective the vista, the less scanning is required to encompass the meaning of place. Amos Rapoport warns, however, that such rules usually ignore the nature of elements viewed, the role of kinesthetics and other sensing modalities, the dynamic nature of visualization, and observer characteristics. In addition, it is often overlooked that both height and distance are subjectively estimated and depend upon the size of the space involved, light conditions (including atmospherics), the overlapping of objects, and height above horizon, among other factors.[15]

Vistas, as limited channels of vision, give rise to the expectation that, should the observation point be moved forward, further vistas might be revealed and the field of vision advanced. The eye, therefore, scans the street for "focal points" to serve as vantage points from which vision can be enhanced. The "primary vantage point" is the location from which a sense of prospect is first achieved. "Secondary vantage points" offer potential prospect. Such focal points, as arrayed along the axis of view, tend to break the primary vista into segments. Indeed, James Barker, Michael Fazin, and Hank Hildebrant, in their analysis of American small town landscapes, argue that each segment of street should have such a point of focus to give it clarity.[16] In the Nantucket scene, the church at the end of the block offers itself as a point of secondary vista (see fig. 3.11). Here one can renew the view ahead, and obtain lateral views as well. Secondary vantage points raise questions as to what lies ahead and thus excite expectations. These expectations create a sense of heightened interest, even a sense of mystery, as the sightseer moves along a street.

The most effective vantage points appear as elevated locations. A tower, such as the church tower in Nantucket, offers a clear sense of vertical dimension. Its high visibility also punctuates the sense of horizontal space, effectively subdividing the vista. Towers arrest the eye's horizontal outreach and exploration. Towers suggest the potential of rising above the street where, freed from an attachment to the ground, panoramas may be seen. Of course, towers have clear symbolic value. They represent a kind of standing up against the forces of gravity because the eye identifies not with the downward pressure of wall upon ground, but with the apparent upward thrust of mass. Peter Smith writes with a degree of hyperbole: "Primordially the tower was a means of escaping from the trials of earthbound reality and approaching the celestial realm. It is an expression of the archetypal appetite for gigantism. By associating with the scale of the supernormal one symbolically casts off the chains of mortality."[17]

Towers provide views down and over landscapes. The view over Caernarfon Castle in Wales illustrates this (fig. 3.12). The viewer obtains what Higuchi calls a satisfying "angle of

Figure 3.12

Towers as elevated vantage
point—Caernarfon Castle,
Wales. Bird's-eye views are of
universal appeal for the
heightened sense of prospect they
convey. The view down on the
castle and the town beyond
subsume a diversity of objects
easily encompassed. The novelty
of the scene invites visual
exploration, a visual experiencing
of things from unusual
perspective. The viewer seems
not to occupy the place seen so
much as to be distanced from it.
The world appears as a model of
itself, miniaturized for ease of
comprehension.

depression" (the angle between the horizontal and the ray
entering the eye from the object being viewed). When standing, one's normal line of vision is about 10 degrees below the
horizontal, and when seated about 15 degrees. Thus to look
slightly downward, as the photograph does, is a normal reflex.
Positions of height that encourage downward viewing are
inherently satisfying up to 30 degrees below the horizontal.
Of course, all of this says nothing about the novelty of seeing
objects from above and the fact that "bird's-eye views" usually
encompass larger areas (and thus superintend greater variety)
than corresponding ground-level views. Elevated viewpoints
introduce degrees of vertical dimension otherwise lacking.[18]

Rise in topographical level also draws the eye. The traditional ascent to the biblical city on the hill has its counterpart in
Birmingham's rebuilt business center (fig. 3.13). "Climbing is
a heroic, liberating act," Arnheim writes, "and height
spontaneously symbolizes things of value, be it the value of
worldly power or of spirituality." To Barker, Fazin, and
Hildebrant, ascending is to go into the unknown. It produces

a "feeling of superiority, exhilaration, and command." Thus in the Birmingham scene the motorist is alert to the unknown that lies ahead still hidden from view. From the successful assault on uncertainty, however, a sense of power can be derived from daring to conquer. Descending, across what Appleton calls "falling ground," produces feelings of inferiority. In the downtown San Francisco scene there is relatively little mystery and the way forward is clearly visible (fig. 3.14). The make-up of the street is known. Cullen writes that below level produces intimacy, inferiority, enclosure, and claustrophobia because the act of descending implies going down into the known. Smith summarizes: horizontal lines represent "equilibrium, stability and control." But, rising lines suggest an "energy-release" and are regarded as "cheerful," whereas descending lines imply a "decline in energy" and are associated with "melancholy."[19]

Constrictions along a street also make excellent vantage points. When, as pictured in Kansas City, a building alignment along one side of a street is projected forward, the way ahead is partially concealed, suggesting at least momentary pause (fig. 3.15). The motorist necessarily slows in anticipation of congested traffic and prepares to look beyond the intersection. By necessity he seeks a secondary vista at this obvious vantage point. A situation where both sides of a street or road are constricted creates a clear venturi effect, as is seen along the Pennsylvania highway shown (fig. 3.16). When movement occurs from a large space through a narrow opening, an in-

Figure 3.14

The view descending—San Francisco, California. To descend is to enter places fully seen and thus fully known. Descent holds little challenge as either a physical or visual act. Views over landscapes are inherently comforting, because one feels a sense of control over that which literally "lies at one's feet." But there is no mystery, for the motorist comprehends fully his trajectory to the base of the hill.

Figure 3.15

Constriction—Kansas City, Missouri. The street constricts from four traffic lanes into two, suggesting difficulty of movement ahead. The building that laterally constricts the vista on the right offers clear punctuation breaking the view into segments. The motorist seeks renewed vista in the street beyond. At the intersection the motorist is also inclined to look laterally, to seek secondary vistas along the streets opening up visually at right angles to his movement.

crease in visual pressure results, similar to the venturi principle of physics. The energy of movement is heightened and anticipation results. Grady Clay considers the "venturi" an important element of landscape because it is "a gatherer, an accumulator, and accelerator of traffic, movement, and information." Smith writes of "vortex space" which creates a special "psychological pull."[20]

A constriction intensifies vision along an original line of sight. However, it may also imply a "lateral vista" when

Figure 3.16

Figure 3.16
Venturi effect—highway near
Green Park, Pennsylvania. Here
the constriction is imposed by
lateral intrusions from both sides
of the roadway, which suggest
not only congestion and slower
movement, but also acceleration
beyond the constriction: a venturi
effect.

associated with a large breach in the confining wall, the breach
suggesting a secondary vista approximately at right angles to
the main vistal channel. The intersection in Kansas City is such
an instance (see fig. 3.15). Such a situation creates an even
stronger inclination to pause and may provide a sense of
security, the lateral opening being a logical place of protection
from the exposure of the street. Appleton uses the French term
coulisse to describe this effect. Originally a theatrical term
denoting scenery projecting from the wings onto a stage, the
term is also applied in art criticism to any lateral projection
from the flanks of a scene.[21] To the yachtsman, headlands suggest viewpoints beyond which secondary vistas obtain, as in
the Trincomali Channel off British Columbia pictured in
figure 3.17.

The successful street as vista forms what might be called
"teleological space."[22] It is a visual array that offers numerous
goals for exploration. The successive disclosures of secondary
vistas give scope to the imagination to invite exploration.
Teleological aesthetics are essentially inductive, with the sightseer moving from vantage point to vantage point to piece
together a total picture of landscape. It is an act of repeated
anticipation and discovery as imagination confronts the realities of place. The successful street as vista integrates various
structural forms toward teleological impulse. The overall
effect is indicative. Movement is motivated with implications
about the hidden beyond.

Redundancies make the strongest visual images. Redundan-

Figure 3.17

Coulisse—Trincomali Channel near Otter Bay, British Columbia. The projection of land on the right suggests a secondary vista, an obvious point of pause, and, perhaps, a place of protection off the main channel of movement.

cies result when various forms reinforce one another toward common visual effect. Appleton calls such reinforcement "reduplication." It is the use of two or more symbols of similar kind to reinforce the same visual effect. For example, the linear character of a highway as vista may be reinforced by parallel power lines, a painted center line, and, indeed, by buildings effectively spaced (fig. 3.18). All these features serve to channel the eyes forward along the road. Such reduplication reinforces the basic sense of linearity suggesting movement. The eye is drawn into the scene with greater intensity. Focal points such as distant farmsteads become aiming points in actual or implied locomotion.[23]

REFUGE

If visualizing landscape is first a search for prospect, then it is next a search for refuge. Refuge, or the sense of security, is implicit in focal points where protection may be obtained. As Appleton argues, this need may not be consciously felt, but may, instead, be subliminal, a relic of biological inheritance. As man the hunter sought both to see and to hide, so the sight-seer not only seeks visual expanse, but security in scenery as well. He seeks aspects of scenery that suggest a stepping out of the active mainstream. The most successful landscapes, there-fore, are seen not only in terms of clearly legible panoramas and vistas, but in terms of places of containment such as

Figure 3.18
Reduplication—highway near
Elliotsburg, Pennsylvania. The
power lines, the center line, and
the position of the barns serve to
strengthen the linear trajectory of
the road. The view forward is
thus reinforced, each component
adding strength to the sense of
forward momentum. The
motorist is pulled into the scene.

coulisses. Above all, the sightseer seeks aspects of scenery that
appear to condense and thus slow the pace of visualization
through the enhancement of enclosure. Implicit is a sense of
hazard avoided.[24]

Enclosures

Spaces completely or nearly contained by surrounding walls
are enclosures, the sense of enclosure obtained from within
rather than from without. Enclosed spaces, as outdoor rooms,
embody, according to Cullen, the idea of "hereness." Looking
out of the enclosure automatically creates a sense of "thereness." The eye reacts to the fact of being surrounded by wall
surfaces. Cullen writes: "The reaction is static: once an
enclosure is entered, the scene remains the same as you walk
across it and out of it, where a new scene is suddenly revealed."
Raymond Curran notes: "The movement of the eye, unlike
with linear spaces, is not directed away from the viewer, but
'around.' The principal effect of the surface relationships is that
of concentrating attention on a distinct and static roomlike
spatial form."[25]

Enclosures function as containers. Simple shapes like
squares, rectangles, and circles permit rapid visual exploration
from a static position and space appears to be efficiently
bounded. Oblong or complicated shapes require more visual
exploration and, generally, more viewer movement as well.
Curran distinguishes between three principal kinds of spatial

Figure 3.19

Spatial enclosure—(a) inverted,
(b) strategic, and (c) compound
spaces are the three principal
types of spatial enclosure.
Modified from Raymond J.
Curran, *Architecture and the Urban
Experience* (New York: Van
Nostrand Reinhold, 1983),
p. 112.

A

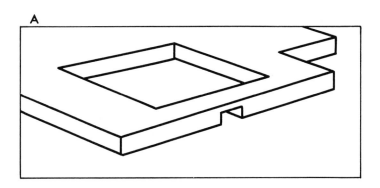

B

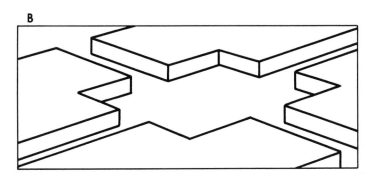

C

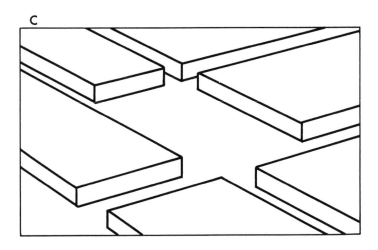

Figure 3.20

Inverted space—London's Somerset House. Entered through an arched portal, this inner courtyard is fully enclosed, giving a sense of complete containment. The traffic of the nearby Strand has little effect. There is visual stability here, the corners and the sides of the square deflecting the eye toward the center. The eye cannot escape the enclosure.

containment: (1) inverted spaces; (2) strategic spaces; and (3) compound spaces (fig. 3.19). Each type varies according to the extent and manner by which surrounding walls are open to the outside.

"Inverted spaces," such as the interior courtyard of London's Somerset House, most closely approximate the interior rooms of buildings (fig. 3.20). They are enclosures without any major breaks in surrounding surfaces. Entered like rooms through portals, the relationship to surrounding area is indirect. The activities of adjacent streets do not flow into or otherwise directly influence the use of these areas. Inverted spaces stand as protected islands of visual stability and the viewer feels contained because moving in the enclosure does not appreciably alter the sense of view.[26]

"Strategic spaces," such as diamond-shaped squares, are central within a street pattern. The activities of connecting streets do flow directly into and out of these enclosures through the openings of each side as shown in the photograph of Savannah, Georgia (fig. 3.21). These breaks create a tension between the sense of containment and the sense of free movement as the eye is easily carried beyond the enclosure along the axes of radiating streets. However, as Ashihara points out, the "inside corners," formed where the sides meet, counter this effect.[27] The eye is abruptly stopped and held by the angles at which the connected sides come together as on the Indiana public square pictured in figure 3.22. Where an object, such as

Figure 3.21
Strategic space—Savannah,
Georgia. Traffic moves in and out
of this square, each side
penetrated by a busy street. Here
the eye easily glances up Bull
Street toward Savannah's city hall
which, with the avenue, forms a
terminated vista, the sense of
containment deriving less from
the square and more from the
vista. Vision escapes the
confinement of the square to be
anchored elsewhere.

Figure 3.22
Inside corner—public square,
Angola, Indiana. The corners of
strategic spaces hold the eye in an
angular cul-de-sac, thus
enhancing the sense of
containment lost in the
penetrated sides. Strategic spaces
mix stability and action as the
confined corners play off against
the penetrated sides.

a monument, defines the center of a strategic space, an especially attractive valence is created between the corners and
the center which appears to anchor the space as pause rather
than release it as movement, as is clearly demonstrated in the
downtown Indianapolis Monument Circle (fig. 3.23).

Perhaps the most successful strategic space is the circular
space with uniform perimeter. Illustrated is the Royal Circus at
Bath, England (fig. 3.24). Such a "square" not only stresses its

Figure 3.23

Defining the center—
Indianapolis, Indiana. The large
Soldiers and Sailors' Monument
provides a definitive anchor for
the city's Monument Circle. A
strong visual tension has been
created between the concave
inside corners and the center.
Although the periphery is
penetrated, it communicates with
strength given the monument's
scale. A strong valence has been
set up between the surrounding
edge and center. Not just the
monument but the circle itself has
become a primary symbol of the
city, so visually successful is this
strategic space.

identity by unbreakable coherence of contour, but it also
establishes its center with compelling precision. From the
center, the square's field of forces expands in all directions and
is confirmed by the concavity of the boundary facades. The
convexity of the square's shape designates it as the dominant
figure, whereas the concave facades recede under the impact of
forces advancing from the center.[28] Enclosed circular spaces
almost demand a central object as focal point to symbolize the
source of the centrifugal forces released.

Finally, "compound spaces" are hybrid enclosures. Streets
pass along two or more sides, allowing space to "leak out" at
the corners.[29] Shown, by way of illustration, is Toronto's City
Hall Plaza (fig. 3.25). As the space is poorly contained, the
sense of enclosure is weakened. The eye easily follows streets
in search of vista. However, when a structure anchors such a
square at the center, the eye may be drawn back into the en-

Figure 3.24

The circle as strategic space—
Bath, England. Circular plazas
with uniformly structured edges,
such as Bath's Royal Circus,
make the most effective strategic
spaces. A field of visual tension
radiates outward from the center
to be confirmed in every direction
by the concavity of the
encompassing building facades.
Here is ultimate visual stability
involving a balance of sensed
centripetal and centrifugal forces.

Figure 3.25

Compound space—Toronto,
Ontario. Traffic passes along
several sides of Toronto's City
Hall Plaza, allowing space to
"leak out" of the corners. Space is
not well contained and the sense
of enclosure is weakened
accordingly. In this view the
plaza stands not so much as a
place of confinement as it stands
as a place of interface with the
surrounding city.

closure because the central focus effects counterposition with
one of the enclosure's sides or with a distant landmark as illustrated by London's Trafalgar Square (fig. 3.26). Trafalgar
Square's visual success derives not from its sense of enclosure
so much as from the valences struck by the Nelson Monument
and other landmarks both near and far.

Not only do the configuration of a space and the manner in
which it is breached influence the sense of enclosure, the

Figure 3.26

Defining the center—London's Trafalgar Square. The Nelson Monument serves to anchor the eye in this compound space. A tension has been set up between the monument, the square's edges, and distant focal points such as the tower of Big Ben glimpsed here. Here also the sense of connection is strong and the sense of containment weak.

size of a space relative to the height of the enclosing walls is also important. This is Greenbie's already mentioned distance/height ratio. Arnheim writes of two kinds of spontaneous space encounter. First, space is seen as a container existing prior to, and independent of, the objects that are contained within. Spaces between objects are seen as merely empty. A second conception suggests that space is created as a relationship between objects. Separating space appears influenced by the objects themselves through a "field of force" seen as surrounding the objects. Buildings of given size and bulk dictate a sense of proper distance to one another. The same rule of conduct also holds for observers in their visual relationships with structures. When an area is too small, it has insufficient space to respond to the pressure of surrounding buildings by generating a vectorial center of its own. When it is too large the dynamic fields of the surrounding buildings do not extend far enough toward the center. By the same token, whatever focus develops at the center cannot spread far enough to engage the boundary, and thereby establish a structural organization throughout the enclosure.[30]

The feeling of enclosure is influenced by the relation of viewing distance to building height. When a facade height equals the distance one stands from a building (a 1 to 1 relationship) the cornice is at a 45 degree angle from the line of forward horizontal sight. Because the building is considerably higher

Figure 3.27

Enclave—Syracuse, New York. Enclaves are interior enclosures easily accessible from outdoor public space. They are cued by entrances that clearly symbolize refuge. Inside the pedestrian is protected from the street, either the whirl of traffic, as at midday, or the danger of abandoned streets, as in the late evening depicted here.

than the upper limit of the field of forward vision (30 degrees), one feels well enclosed. When a facade height equals one-half the distance over which it is being viewed (1 to 2) it coincides with the 30 degree upper limit of normal vision. This Spreiregen calls the "threshold of distraction," the lower limit for creating a feeling of enclosure. When facade height equals one-third the distance from the building (1 to 3), the top is seen at about an 18 degree angle enabling objects to be seen beyond the space itself. The space has lost its containing quality.[31]

Enclaves

Refuge may be had at various scales. Enclosures such as public squares are large scale and may contain masses of people. What Cullen calls an "enclave," however, is small scale. It is an invitation of refuge to relatively small numbers of people. Enclaves can nest within the confines of enclosures as they also nest along the linear expanses of streets. To Cullen, an enclave is an interior space open to the exterior having free and direct access one to the other. In the photograph from downtown Syracuse, enclave is variously implied (fig. 3.27). The overhang of sidewalk canopy and pedestrian bridge creates a sense of enclosure out of which the pedestrian at street level peers. Across and down the street, doorways beckon offering entrance to interior spaces. Ideally, an enclave is a fully enclosed space with ceiling, as well as walls and floor, well out

Figure 3.28

Enclave—Cleveland, Ohio. An arcade invites pedestrians off a public street and into protected confines. In this view, a second order of enclave exists in the individual shop entrances which invite pedestrians off the arcade's concourse. A hierarchy of enclaves welcomes the shopper into not only an ordered but also a protected world.

of the directional mainstream of travel. It is a place apart conceived of as a position of safety.[32] The Cleveland Arcade pictured represents a classic use of enclave in commercial retail development (fig. 3.28). Not only is the arcade itself a place of refuge connecting Cleveland's Superior and Euclid streets, but shops open off its interior atrium as enclaves defined at a lesser scale. As an interior space cannot be seen from the outside, its character in landscape is only symbolized by its openings to the outside, especially the elaboration (or lack of elaboration) of entrance as invitation. Enclaves are focal points of obvious resort as the sightseer moves down a street or around a square. They offer immunity from exposure, a kind of cover.

The character of a landscape is largely determined by its degree of "openness." The solidity or transparency of the boundaries of a space make the space appear either isolated or part of a more comprehensive totality. Architect Robert

Figures 3.29 and 3.30
Large and small entrances—
Chicago's Loop and New York
City's Brooklyn Heights. Large
entrances imply large, public
interior spaces. Small entrances
imply small, private interiors. A
downtown movie theater must
announce itself in grand terms to
entice a clientele. Here the classic
arch writ large invites the public.
Entrances to houses may make
overtures to status by use of the
classic arch as well, but size
announces that these are private
spaces. The nature of enclave and
the appropriate behaviors
contained is made clear.

Venturi writes: "Architecture occurs at the meeting of interior
and exterior forces of use and space. This meeting is expressed
in walls and, more specifically, in the particular openings in
walls which connect exterior forces of use and space." Where
windows are many the interior space is symbolized as more
public than private. Where an entrance is large the interior
space is perceived as large rather than small (figs. 3.29 and
3.30). However perceived, entrances signal "enclave" as a
place of pause. Arnheim writes: "Instead of leaving the occu-
pant in a boundless world, an interior encloses him like a
womb. . . . The world of interior can be totally encompassed;
it is surveyable, more nearly relatable than the outside to the
size and power of a human being, and is therefore susceptible
to his domination."[33]

The appearance of enclaves along a street, Ashihara notes, is
a function of yet another ratio: that of building width to street
width. Where building width regularly exceeds street width

there appears a general paucity of enclaves. A street in Taos, New Mexico, provides illustration (fig. 3.31). The lack of entrance propels the eye forward across a blank facade which dominates the street: length of wall overpowering width of street. There is no refuge here until the public square is reached beyond. Treatment of the so-called zone of transition, which ties inside and outside symbolically together, is another important factor cueing refuge. The outdoor café is an excellent example of transitional space organized both functionally and visually to draw people off the street toward an interior situation (fig. 3.32). The café is an invitation to rest just out of the swirl of pedestrian and motorized traffic and from there to view the world in the relative safety of quiet contemplation. As Yi-Fu Tuan notes, the appeal of cities lies in large part on the "juxtaposition of the cozy and the grand, of darkness and light, the intimate and the public." Enclave, epitomized by the sidewalk café, is the very essence of that juxtaposition.[34]

Figure 3.31

Paucity of enclave—Taos, New Mexico. There is no sense of refuge evident in this expanse of uninterrupted adobe wall. The eye is carried steadily forward to the square beyond where porticoes and shop entrances announce enclave. The walk is sterile in contrast to the visual excitement of the square.

Figure 3.32

Zone of transition— Niagara-on-the-Lake, Ontario. The glass of this café provides a clear transition between outside and inside. The entrance draws people off the street and into a fully exposed enclave. The view outward is from the protection of chair and table, well outside the swirl of traffic. The view inward is from the bustling sidewalk and street toward quiet repose. The two worlds meet and mix in the glass reflection.

Points of Pause

Enclosures invite pause in movement as sightseers find themselves closed-in. Enclaves, in suggesting interior refuge, are also diversions from movement. There is a third form of refuge as yet unnamed in the literature. It is what I call the "point of pause." It is an island of safety in the mainstream of movement, or a protected eddy beside the mainstream. The point of pause is not enclosed. Physically, it is cued by a clearly demarcated "floor" which invites observers to pause in their movement. It may be a pedestrian island in the middle of a busy street, as pictured in Philadelphia (fig. 3.33). There pedestrians scramble for safety. Or it may be a "pullout," a "lay-by," or an "aire de repos" for motorists as pictured

Figure 3.33

Point of pause—streetcar stop in Philadelphia, Pennsylvania. A pedestrian island serves as refuge on a busy commercial avenue. Here is a safe place in the scheme of movement connecting the potentialities of walking and riding. For those merely crossing the street, the island offers potential safety from vehicular traffic.

Figure 3.34

Point of pause—highway turnout near Corgaff Castle, Scotland. Here is an opportunity to survey the landscape outside the flow of traffic. The motorists' view of landscape is influenced by such a realization whether or not they avail themselves of the opportunity to stop.

along a roadside in Scotland (fig. 3.34). It is a point at which pedestrians feel they can stand back outside the swirl of movement and not be carried along; it is a point at which motorists feel they can pull out of traffic for temporary rest.

Space can be separated into zones for movement or for rest. Movement spaces are dynamic, carrying the eye constantly forward, whereas rest spaces are static, allowing the eye to pause and study.[35] Points of pause are static, but they take on meaning not to the extent that they are used, but to the extent that they have the potential for use. They are recognized and valued as a means of reducing hazard in movement. Because a point of pause is not cued by physical structure so

Figures 3.35, 3.36, and 3.37
Serial vision—Dallas, Texas.
Views are supplanted by
emerging views in a constant
round of seeing that is serial
vision. Here the highway directs
the eye forward past buildings
only seen peripherally in passing.

much as by the use of space, it stands as the weakest of the various forms of refuge. The most significant points of pause in the sightseer's composition of views are linked with vantage points, the pause used as an opportunity to enhance vision. Again, points of pause function primarily in the sightseer's world to offer reassurance. Whether the sightseer actually uses a refuge or not, awareness of it conveys assurance through a sense of potential security.

SERIAL VISION

Sightseers seek views of landscapes that variously combine aspects of prospect and refuge. Viewing landscape is not a static proposition because landscapes are inherently spatio-

temporal in their organization. Their conceptualization
requires a dynamic orientation. Streets, even individual buildings, unfold to view over time, cueing place meaning
temporally as objects come into view and disappear. Landscape appears to emerge and occlude. Landscapes are read
piecemeal over time. Arnheim writes: "This perspective unfolding is an essential part of the experience that transforms the
simultaneity of space into a sequence in time. As we walk or
drive, the environment becomes a happening, in which things
follow one another and change shape while they change
position."[36]

Sightseeing as a search for satisfying scenes is very much a
process of serial vision, sightseers seeking visual novelty
through sequences of revelation. Existing views are supplanted by emerging views in an unfolding visual drama.
Figures 3.35, 36, and 37 show a sequence of photographs along
a Dallas freeway shot through an automobile windshield. Place
becomes a high-speed continuous thing, a sequence of related
parts. Space is not isolated or chopped up but is part of a continuous pattern. As a visually successful landscape, there is
a sense of continuity here where one thing seems to lead to the
next. The eye is actively interested in pursuing the tantalizing
juxtapositions. Perhaps there is an analogy to music here
where events along a path relate melodically. Perhaps the
visually successful landscape unfolds classically in a sequence
of introduction, development, climax, and conclusion.

Traditionally, serial vision has been conceptualized as a

sequence of discrete visual images. People in motion, it has been thought, visualize landscape as a sequence of visual fields analogous to still pictures. Gibson rejects this view. Observers who are moving do not see the world at any one point of observation. Rather, they see the world at many points. Views emerge and occlude simultaneously with objects fading-in and fading-out of view cognitively structured as continuous visual sensation. He writes: "A path does not have to be treated as an infinite set of successive instants; it can be thought of as a unitary movement, an excursion, a trip, a voyage." The sight-seer, Gibson would argue, maintains an ever-changing visual image of landscape based on hypotheses of invariant structure. The eye sweeps over the visual array with progressive gain and loss at its leading and trailing edges, and the ambient structure remains invariant. What Gibson does not ask, however, is how sightseers conceptualize invariancy. To what extent do "still" images enter the remembering of scenes actually seen in such transition?[37]

Many architects have called for the design of landscapes based on the principles of serial vision. Lawrence Halprin, for example, sees the essence of urban experience as a process of movement through a sequential and variegated series of spaces. He writes: "Thus, the beautiful street is beautiful—not only because of the fixed objects which line it—but also because of the meaningful relationships it generates for the person-in-motion. His movement is the purpose for the space, and it should function to activate his kinesthetic experience in a series of interesting rhythms and variation in speed and force." Regarding the pedestrian in the city, he concludes: "The qualities of . . . passing under arches and through build-ings, of narrowing and widening of spaces, of long and closed views, of stopping and starting are qualities which make a vital urban experience for the walker and his mobile point of view."[38]

Movement by automobile creates its own design possibili-ties. Not only is the speed of motion faster, but the surround-ing vehicle appears immobile. It is only the displacement of the things beyond that confirm for the eyes the kinesthetic information of locomotion. Planners Donald Appleyard, Kevin Lynch, and John Meyer studied the essence of serial vision implicit in automobile travel, although their concern was not the landscape as visualized so much as the visualized landscape as recalled or remembered. Their findings were set forth in the now classic monograph, *The View from the Road*. The motorist's view of the urban expressways studied was highly restricted. The car interposed a filter between the driver and the world, his vision framed and limited largely to a forward view. Compared to pedestrians, drivers were relatively inactive, with little opportunity to stop, explore, or choose paths, although feelings of speed and grace of movement compensated for these limitations. Drivers necessarily watched the changing scene constantly, their vision confined to a narrow angle of view focused on the road itself. Passengers were freer to look or not look and enjoyed a wider angle of vision less concerned with the road and immediate traffic.[39]

Trips were reconstructed primarily on the basis of the objects seen, and the manner by which objects appeared to be sequenced in the kaleidoscope of sequential views. Two-thirds of these objects were in or adjacent to the road itself and appeared themselves to be moving, especially the objects of the near roadside seen peripherally. Periods of wide scanning were infrequent and tied primarily to turns in the road and changes of grade where route decisions were required. However, attention always returned quickly to the road: the road defining the prevailing vistas. Landscape visualization was modified by speed. They write: "As speed increases, attention is confined to a narrower forward angle, since coming events must be predicted further ahead. As near objects rush past more rapidly, they are harder to perceive and attention may shift to more distant and relatively more stable elements. Landmarks are seen in clusters rather than singly; larger spaces and bigger landforms take command. The scene shifts from detail to generality." Where surrounding objects were few, far off, or unarticulated, a sensation of floating or of no forward movement prevailed. Conversely, where the near environment held many highly articulated objects, the sensation was one of great velocity.[40]

The road was conceptualized as a sequence to be followed, and thus itself was seen as moving through the landscape. Objects welled up and fell behind, broke in two as they passed overhead, slipped sidewise, or rotated. Apparent motions became intricate dances when groups of objects were seen together. Landmarks moved against a background or a foreground, were caught in a moving frame, were masked and revealed, or rotated first one way and then another. Most trips were goal oriented; that is, observers had a sense of moving from one focal point to another through succeeding vistas. Vistas followed each other as in simple chains or were seen to overlap. Nearby focal points were passed with distant ones still within sight; or, distant focal points, seen and then obscured, were revealed once again in a sequence of vista gained, lost, and regained.[41]

The View from the Road has only limited applicability to our concern with sightseeing. First, the subjects studied were not sightseers, but were commuters long familiar with the expressways traversed. Second, views were not analyzed so much as the memories of views visible from the road. Third, the authors were primarily concerned with objects as landmarks. They tabulated sets of objects remembered. They did not attempt to reconstruct the manner by which objects were seen to arrange in scenes. By restricting themselves to the study of expressway driving, they largely ignored the importance of enclosure and enclave in landscape. It is true, as they assert, that travel on urban expressways is a new way of making the structure of vast cities comprehensible to the eye. A city can be differentiated and related by motorists from expressway vantage points, although cities can only be comprehended in their broadest outlines. Obviously, techniques similar to those employed by Appleyard, Lynch, and Meyer need to be applied in the study of other kinds of urban trip-taking on other kinds of urban paths.

Speed of movement clearly influences what is visualized in landscape. High speed can make a single landscape seem more complex, whereas slow speed can make a complex landscape seem simple. As speed increases, visualization becomes more demanding and calls for voluntary attention. What the mind can handle may very well be remembered as a series of still pictures representing a disjointed conceptualization of landscape. According to Rapoport, the point of concentration or focus recedes from 600 feet at twenty-five mph to 2,000 feet at sixty-five mph. As a result, objects must be larger to command attention. Peripheral vision diminishes. Whereas at twenty-five mph the horizontal angle of the field of view is 100 degrees, it reduces to less than 40 degrees at sixty mph to produce a kind of "tunnel vision." Foreground detail fades due to the perceived rapid movement of close objects. The closest point of clear view recedes from 30 feet at forty mph to 110 feet at sixty mph. At that speed, detail beyond 1,400 feet cannot be seen because it is too small. Thus the range of focus is between approximately 110 and 1,400 feet at sixty mph, a distance traversed in only fifteen seconds. Near objects are seen, get close, and disappear very quickly. They loom and vanish rapidly.[42]

In searching landscape for meaningful cues to scenic place, the myriad objects in view may readily overwhelm, especially in an urban situation of high-speed movement. Thus anticipations in the face of landscape complexity are made necessarily simple, the vast majority of the available cues filtered out in favor of those that validate generalized expectations. The search for prospect, the recognition of vistas of varying character, for example, is one way in which simplification may occur. The search for refuge, the recognition of enclosure, enclave, and point of pause, similarly may provide a sense of landscape integration. Comprehending landscape may be, therefore, a piecing together of views given meaning through quests for prospect and refuge. Serial vision is not a mere cataloging of objects seen in sequence. Where the elements of prospect and refuge combine in unexpected ways to provide an overall framework for visualization, visually satisfying landscapes are experienced. From the sightseer's point of view, these are the views that stand out involuntarily to hold attention, and set, as image, a template for anticipating succeeding views in the search for place meaning. The highly stimulating views that linger in the mind set expectations for the sequential knowing of a place as scenery. Spontaneous sightseeing is cyclical with periods of intense attention followed by periods of less attention lapsing even into inattention when sensory adaptation sets in. A highly stimulating view excites alertness to that which follows and, thereby, resets the sequence of enhanced expectation and awareness. Space-covering search becomes place-organizing search.

A landscape may be deliberately or inadvertently structured to excite or reset visual attention. Especially exciting views may offer a sense of "announcement." It is a first impression combining a vantage point and a vista with a set of succeeding focal points as prospect. It often is enhanced further by a sense

Figure 3.38

Announcement—highway at Mosher, South Dakota. Expectations are created when a grain elevator comes into view announcing another town. "Here I am," the motorist muses, "and there is the next town." It is a first impression based on a panorama structured by the reduplication of road and power lines carrying the eye from focal point to focal point toward the town as goal.

of enclosure as goal, with enclaves and points of pause presenting intervening opportunities for refuge. An announcement may give a sense of entry or exit into a frame of place meaning, as in the South Dakota photograph (fig. 3.38). The highway, visually reinforced by parallel power lines and fence, sweeps down into a valley, where a small town offers refuge ahead: its grain elevator a clear focal point in the panorama disclosed. Brought suddenly to view at the crest of a ridge, the town is announced with some drama. Here is a sense of counterposition which contrasts a strong "foreground of hereness" with a strong "background of thereness."[43]

The sightseer's view of landscape is structured in broad outline by the search for prospect and refuge. Experience is emerging and occluding panoramas, vistas, focal points, enclosures, enclaves, and points of pause combined to offer scenery as visual interest. Sometimes it entails the dramatic juxtapositioning of such visual elements. However, visual interest does not reside alone in broad outlines of landscape. It resides as well in the small-scale textures of the material world. Visual interest also resides in the character of place contributed by the myriad of objects, animate and inanimate, which relate as visual detail. In the next chapter I turn to the sense of character in place which detailed seeing brings to landscape visualization. I ask: What kinds of drama do detailed articulations bring to sightseeing as place experience?

Chapter 4

Character
in
Landscape

Reality only reveals itself
when illuminated by a ray of
poetry.

GEORGES BRAQUE

Sightseers thrive on place images rich in detail. Scenes broadly
outlined are enhanced as the tourists' eyes seek character in
place. In part, they search for scale: the relevancy of man, or of
man and machine, in the built environment. They search for
appropriateness or the suitability of elements in the larger
milieu. They attempt to put a face on the landscape in order to
personify place. They respond to the peculiarities of light,
especially color. Character brings to a scene the distinctiveness
of object and spatial order that stamps a particular place as truly
unique. It cues what Lawrence Durrell calls "the spirit of
place," and what other authors variously refer to as "personality of place" and "sense of place." It is obtained not so much
from moving through a landscape as by stopping and watching
a place in its many manifestations. Durrell writes of sightseeing: "It is a pity indeed to travel and not get this essential
sense of landscape values. One does not need a sixth sense for it
because all landscapes ask the same question: 'I am watching
you—are you watching yourself in me?' "[1]

75

Character of place is as much a matter of quiet introspection as of seeing. It is a personal identification with the objects of place. It may result in an affective tie with the material environment, or in what Yi-Fu Tuan calls "topophilia." Ian Nairn comments: "It seems commonplace that almost everyone is born with the need for identification with his surroundings and a relationship to them—with the need to be in a recognizable place." Thus sense of place is not a fine-arts extra, he argues, because it is, in fact, something people cannot do without. Places, he concludes, should be designed to elicit identification whereby the individual inserts himself emotionally into a scene. Christian Norberg-Schultz implies that such identifications can be passed from individual to individual as a kind of cultural rootedness. He writes of genius loci whereby every place has its "guardian spirit" which influences people in their determination of place character. Places, he argues, elicit characterization from people.[2]

The search for character involves interpreting the objects of place as symbols of human intent. Place meanings encourage or discourage sightseers according to behavioral expectations. A place elicits distinctive ways of being from those who occupy it regularly. Tourists, as sightseers, can learn to sense these styles, and, indeed, be influenced by them. Sightseers should know that a place into which they have wandered has meaning significant in terms of humanity as well as aesthetics. Sightseers should seek to capture its peculiar flavor, its nuances, if they can. Character, Henry Canby writes, "will prove to be, like style in literature, the most imponderable quality, never to be defined and never to be neglected, which when found or felt is a new clue not merely to beauty, but to subject, significance, mood, and result."[3]

SCALE

Human scale is the sense that places belong to people, that the objects of place are person oriented.[4] Scale in architecture is appropriately defined when building components relate harmoniously to the human form, building up, as it were, from the pedestrian in the street. In the view of New York City's Park Avenue, people, vehicles, street furnishings, and buildings (especially those with set-back facades) appear to

Figure 4.1

Sense of scale—New York City's
Park Avenue. A place is said to
express human scale when human
beings can relate to it visually:
structural forms increasing in size
so that an individual feels
comfortable in his surroundings.

build by stages from small to larger scale (fig. 4.1). Visually,
the eye is able to relate the whole by degrees. Such hierarchical
subordination aids the viewer in gauging the size of large
objects. A building attains its size by presenting a hierarchy of
subdivisions, which lead from small units to progressively
larger ones. Buildings do not simply have size but acquire it as
the eyes move from the small units to larger and larger ones,
until the size of the whole can be measured perceptually by the
scale that has been traversed.[5] Huge as a building may be, it can
make contact with a viewer by providing a range of sizes, some
small enough to be clearly relatable to the human form. Where
no such effort is made to relate a building to the person in the
street, it may overpower and appear alien, as implied in the
Boston scene (fig. 4.2). The sign says "Where's Boston?"
Where, indeed, is the human city in this concentration of
high-rise towers soaring abruptly from the narrow streets?

A sense of scale also operates where parts of a city integrate

Figure 4.2

Sense of scale—Boston, Massachusetts. High-rise buildings that loom directly from the street may alienate the pedestrian. A person with preferences for more intimate settings may well wonder, as the sign asks, "Where's Boston?" Here there are no visual guides to scale people to buildings

hierarchically so that people can comprehend a relationship to a geographic whole. Landscapes properly scaled impart feelings of adequacy. The person feels big enough, powerful enough, identifiable enough to be comfortable in the surroundings. The automobile with its speed and personal control is one means of establishing a sense of scale in the modern city. At the very least it begins to neutralize the disparity in size between a person and a city defined by big buildings and large spaces. Travel by automobile quickly brings disparate parts of a city into close proximity. Contrasts are made more vivid. Hierarchical expression in urban space may reflect in the increasing size of buildings as one approaches a city center. The tone of buildings may change to express enhanced status; they may involve greater formality in design and an increase in the density of visual events. Such clues to hierarchy are presented rapidly to view from the moving car and, thereby, the whole is made readily comprehensible.[6]

Figures 4.3, 4.4, and 4.5
Changing scales—New Orleans,
Louisiana. The eye jumps from
scale to scale as it searches for
place meaning. First the street, or
square, then the facades of
buildings, and then the details of
building design. The visually
successful setting, i.e., the scenic
place, readily combines objects
defined at different scales into a
coherent whole. There are no
disjunctures as the eye moves
from scale to scale in search of
visual satisfaction. As the
pedestrian strolls into and
through Jackson Square, a sense
of scenic integrity is knit together
at and across different scales of
comprehension in the sequence of
experience that is serial vision.

Landscapes may be understood at many scales. Most people view cities on at least four levels: on the scale of the entire city, the scale of the street, the scale of the individual building, and the scale of specific architectural elements. The eye jumps from scale to scale as it searches landscape for meaning. The mind lingers at given levels to organize a sense of place. The mind also searches for hierarchical linkage whereby objects and places defined at one scale relate to those defined at another. Thus in Jackson Square in New Orleans the particulars of a set of windows may be seen to relate to a building's overall design, the building to fit into a square or street, the street to fit within a larger areal frame (figs. 4.3, 4.4, and 4.5). Detail is thus

a function of scale: ideally, the detail of one scale summing to synthesize at another.

SEEING IN DETAIL

The search for character of place invites the sightseer to look beneath a landscape's broad outline to study the particular aspects of scenery. Gordon Cullen calls this process "seeing in detail." He believes that the eye must be trained to this kind of subtle seeing because it does not develop without deliberate effort. To Kevin Lynch, on the other hand, such comprehension is a function of familiarity because observers, as their familiarity with a place increases, seem to depend less and less on gross physical continuities to organize the whole, and to delight more and more in specific contrast and uniqueness which vivify a scene. However and whenever acquired, seeing in detail vastly enhances landscape experience as the sightseer, as observer, comes to savor the nuances of place distinctiveness. He savors differences and similarities and the rhythms that they create. He savors the sense of relationship which small and often trivial objects evoke as they play, one against another.[7]

One could offer a litany of the myriad of objects that might conceivably comprise detail in any given place. Instead, I offer a brief discussion of selected categories of detail defined at the scale of the street: street furnishings, pavement, and vegeta-

Figure 4.6

Street furniture—Baltimore, Maryland. Light fixtures, bollards, planters, benches, and other furnishings help to integrate visually Baltimore's inner harbor area. Such details at the scale of the street help establish place character, differentiating one place from another.

tion. These categories have attracted much attention from landscape architects and architects intent on amplifying place meaning through the design of place detail. Architect Lawrence Halprin, for example, sees urban space only as an envelope within which events happen. A city, like a stage set, demands modulators for people in motion. Thus objects for use, comfort, and artistry may be inserted into a place to guide activity. They are small scaled-down objects that, as they are constantly seen, carry visual importance. For example, street furnishings can be made essential to the sense of place that a street conveys. Much of the visual success of Baltimore's renovated waterfront is the result of light fixtures, benches, planters, signs, kiosks, pieces of sculpture, and bollards all placed in careful juxtaposition (fig. 4.6). Street furnishings serve as second-rank foci in the place-organizing search. They serve as dividing elements to break spaces into segments such that varied scales of place experience might obtain.[8]

Pavements function in much the same way. Pictured are two very different places, the differences substantially communicated in the character of pavement (figs. 4.7 and 4.8). Albany's Empire State Plaza is a vast new space broken down to human scale through use of brick terraced and arrayed in various designs. What could be a large impersonal, monotonous surface becomes fine tuned for close-up viewing. But, above all, Empire State Plaza speaks of newness echoed in the crisp pat-

Figure 4.7
Pavement—Empire State Plaza, Albany, New York. Pavements can be used to divide large spaces into visually pleasing sections. Here the eye is teased by complementing textures.

Figure 4.8
Pavement—Nantucket, Massachusetts. The cobblestone streets of this former whaling port not only create a distinctive sensation under foot, but also help define a visual sense of historical ambience. History thus impresses as physical sensation through texture both seen and felt.

terns the brick imbibes. Nantucket's cobblestone streets speak of age, texture suggesting antiquity or persistence over time. There are no contrasts to imply shifts in scale. Rather, the homogeneity of surface implies a larger space than is actually at hand.

The floor underfoot is a very immediate and personal kind of experience for pedestrians. It is both visual and tactile, contributing to what Kent Bloomer and Charles Moore call "haptic sensing." Thus a place may be known for its physical impress underfoot as well as for its visual qualities, the haptic dimension even challenging the visual for primacy.[9] Designers

Figure 4.9
Pavement—Christ Church
College, Oxford, England. Here
pavements of contrasting texture
are used to channel movement.
Pavement texture also serves to
amplify the sense of vista in this
view. The pedestrian is drawn
into the courtyard beyond.

can use pavements of varied physical texture, color, and patterning to guide movement by channeling choice of direction
and preventing encroachment, as pictured at Oxford's Christ
Church College (fig. 4.9). Pavement can be used, as in this
instance, to augment vistas, directing the eye as well as the
body. Visually effective detail not only fills in the basic outline
of scenery, but enhances it. The careful use of street furniture
and pavement can pull an otherwise diverse scene into a unified
visual whole. Such details can reduplicate the larger elements
of a scene.

Vegetation, especially trees and shrubs, also functions to
focus and tie. Vegetation can variously screen, connect, or
emphasize adjacent objects. In the Country Club Plaza area of
Kansas City, street trees are used to reinforce street vistas by
reduplicating and enframing the motorist's view (fig. 4.10).
As the trees branch across the pavement they appear to reduce
street width, bringing opposite building facades closer.

Figure 4.10

Vegetation in an urban setting—
Country Club Plaza, Kansas
City, Missouri. Here shade trees
reduplicate and enframe the
thoroughfare to emphasize the
street as vista, seemingly pulling
buildings on opposite sides of the
street closer together. Foliage also
screens facades to soften
architecture.

Figure 4.11

Trees in the foreground—
Mobile, Alabama. Trees close at
hand have individual character.
The relationship of a person to
tree is not totally visual as sound
(the wind in the leaves) and even
smell (the odor of wet leaves)
enter into the experiencing of a
scene. Visually, one can become
preoccupied with a tree's peculiar
parts: the texture of its trunk, the
pattern of its spreading branches,
the reflective quality of its leaves.

Vegetation can also stand by itself to offer important visual
effect. In the city, trees give people a contact with nature, and,
visually, they serve to soften the hard, unyielding surfaces of
urban construction. Vegetation adds substantially to rural
scenes where everything except sky and water may appear as
vegetation, with the topography only suggested beneath a
cloak of greenery.

Tadahiko Higuchi emphasizes the changing visual contribu-
tions that trees make to views when seen at varying distances.
As foreground, trees are recognizable as individual objects
(fig. 4.11). The leaves, trunks, and branches are discernible as

Figure 4.12

Trees in the middleground—
Terrace Bay, Ontario. In the
middle distance the forest
produces a general texture against
which individual trees may offer
contrast. The eye searches for
general patterns: the contrast of
different species mixed or the
contrast of trees of different age.

belonging to particular trees, and a person is able to relate the size of each tree to his own height. Trees are seen to vary by size, shape, fullness, and material texture of leaf, among other qualities. All of these characteristics impart character to place. In the middle-distance, the outline of trees is visible but details are not (fig. 4.12). "At this range," Higuchi writes, "the trees are too distant to be sensed as units, although they form the texture of the visible surface; trees or clumps of trees of different varieties are perceived as spots within the texture." In the far distance, contours of treetops cannot be seen. The eye only observes major topographic features such as valleys or ridges. Atmospheric conditions may generalize further, vegetation appearing only as an abstract uniformity in terms of color and visual texture (fig. 4.13).[10]

STYLE

Seeing in detail is noting subtle aspects of place and relating them in a test of fitness or appropriateness. How does detail serve to make a place complete? How does detail break a place down into place segments of lesser scale? Again, seeing in detail is, as well, a search for mutual dependence between part and whole. It is a search for a visual grammar whereby details are seen to sum to something where the whole is greater than the parts. It is also a search for style in landscape. Style, implying a characteristic arrangement of things, is readily recognized, when encountered, as following a well-established

Figure 4.13

Trees in the far distance—Near
Monteagle, Tennessee. Here
trees cloak the most distant hills.
Only the topography shows in
the curves of valley and ridge, the
peculiar character of the forest
totally submerged. This
background vegetation serves
only to establish a horizon against
which trees in the foreground and
middleground contrast.

pattern. Style, as architect Roger Scruton notes, is not an
ordered accumulation of detail, but is, rather, a "fitting
deployment." Norberg-Schultz has classified places reflecting
the way in which details combine. He groups landscapes into
three principal style classes: romantic, classical, and cosmic.
Vegetation, pavement, street furnishings, and, indeed, all the
other aspects of detail in place unite variously to dictate a
distinctive kind of placeness varying from landscapes of
extreme variety and complexity, to varied but ordered landscapes, to ordered landscapes with little diversity.[11]

Romantic landscapes are distinguished by extreme variety
and complexity. They are not unified to form simple, univocal
spaces, but are visually complex and seemingly subjective.
Such landscapes are difficult to predict in their multiplicity.
The European medieval town provides archetypal romantic
landscape with its narrow winding streets, hodge-podge of
building forms, and limited formal open spaces (fig. 4.14). So
also does the English garden present a romantic face (fig. 4.15).
Space appears topological rather than geometrical. Basic
configurations are dense and indeterminant and objects often
appear irrational in their positioning due to the multiplication
of members, variation in particulars, and introduction of free
ornament.[12] The lack of simple overriding order makes for
heightened visual interest. Most sightseers find such landscapes visually rewarding. Romantic places in their detail
stimulate as they beckon.

Figure 4.14

Romantic landscape—Ledbury, England. The European medieval town with its irregular streets, varied architecture, and lack of symmetry suggests romance. Such landscape is not easily predicted and thus excites the imagination. Curiosity as to what lies ahead entices the pedestrian down this street. The scene is suggestive, but what lies ahead remains unknown.

Such words as *spontaneity, tension, contraposition, juxtaposition,* and *randomness* define romanticism in landscape. To Halprin, spontaneity provides random and unforeseen opportunities or "those chance occurrences and happenings which are so vital to be aware of—the strange and beautiful which no fixed, preconceived order can produce." Positive tension, according to James Barker and his colleagues, implies a spark of visual energy jumping between nearby elements. Such tension stops short of confusion to excite and maintain curiosity. To Jay Appleton, such "contraposition," the opposite of reduplication, is the playing off of objects as symbols of contrasting type. Contraposition, when seemingly spontaneous, can create positive tension. Cullen calls it "juxtaposition." Juxtaposition, he writes, produces "its own form of drama which will exist inside the overall spatial framework." It is a "marriage of opposites" in its most profound form. Differences seem counterposed randomly.[13]

Figure 4.15

Romantic landscape—Stourhead Garden in England's Wiltshire. The English landscape garden with its irregularity and lack of symmetry echoes the medieval town as a stimulus to visual exploration. A sense of mystery derives from the juxtaposing of varied parts. The visitor is drawn through the garden, never certain of what lies ahead.

Surprise and mystery are key elements in the romantic appeal of landscape. Each requires an overall frame of reference in which unexpected deviations occur. The confusions must be small regions in a visible whole. Surprise involves anomalies that deviate from the anticipated to frustrate expectations in some modest degree. Expectations must not be overly frustrated or confusion rather than surprise results. Tension must be positive because complete chaos without hint of connection is never pleasurable. Mystery exists when a scene promises more information than it actually reveals. The promise of information causes a response, a heightened involvement with the place. Mystery simply implies an unknown element: something that is not fully comprehensible at the present position of time and space. It invites the observer to explore further. Assessing detail for appropriateness provides the mechanism for reducing the complexity of a landscape's puzzle.[14]

Figure 4.16
Classical landscape—Royal
Naval Hospital at Greenwich,
England. The Renaissance
brought a rebirth of classical
symmetry, echoed here at
Greenwich. Each element forms
a part of a family of elements. The
whole is totally balanced and
clearly more than the sum of its
parts. The parts are easily
anticipated one from another as
they nest within a coherent
frame. Prediction derives from a
comprehension of the system as a
whole.

Figure 4.17
Classical landscape—formal
garden at Blenheim Palace,
Woodstock, England. Strict
symmetry underlies Renaissance
garden design. Geometry
prevails ever balanced: forms
replicated by formula. The eye is
not invited to explore an
unknown, but to pleasure in
ready predictability. The visitor
moves to validate expectations.

Classical landscapes are distinguished by clearly intelligible
compositions. Meaningful order has been brought to bear on
the arrangement—often geometric—of objects, as pictured at
Greenwich and Blenheim, England (figs. 4.16 and 4.17). All
the parts have their individual identity, but, at the same time,
they explain the general character of the whole as they coalesce.
Each element forms part of a family of elements as place is
defined as an additive group. Such words as *simplicity, balance,*
and *harmony* define classicism in landscape. Simplicity is a
limitation of parts. Even when parts are many they are

Figure 4.18

Rectilinear street grid—San Francisco, California. A classic grid of streets has been imposed on the rugged topography of the San Francisco Peninsula. Thus the flat regularity seen in most North American cities is here relieved by exaggerated vertical relief, making San Francisco one of the most imageable cities in the world. Classicism provides a norm upon which the vertical differences of topographic relief and tall buildings foist surprise.

subordinated to the whole in order to attract minimal notice. The observer is invited to distort the complex facts into simple forms. Balance appears when things seem to cohere into a picture of equilibrium, and everything has come to a visual standstill. No change seems possible and the whole assumes the character of necessity in all of its parts because nothing can be added or taken away without destroying the harmony of the whole. Classicism involves the use of satisfying proportions. Indeed, mathematical relations may be used to produce a sense of visual harmony as, for example, the Golden Section of classical Greece, which exhibits the ratio $(1 + \sqrt{5}):2$. An architect may take some such basic measure or module from which to derive all lengths and forms in a building's facade. The parts of the facade will then of necessity stand to each other in direct and harmonious relationship.[15]

The American city offers archetypal classical landscape. It is a carpentered world replete with straight lines, right angles, and rectangular objects. It is a world dominated by what Nairn calls "axial formality" as streets stretch to horizons as straight lines. It is a world of axes meeting at right angles, and the street grid so formed is everywhere dominant as an integrating mechanism easily conceptualized. Even San Francisco on its very hilly site displays the classic grid (fig. 4.18). Such townscapes are comprised of individual formal gestures which sum to an ideal. The overall conception is very simple. It appears

Figure 4.19

Cosmic landscape—Grand Canyon National Park, Arizona. No landscape appears more "cosmic" than the Grand Canyon: a seemingly infinite space of eroded rock and glaring sun. It is a repetition of sculptured rock carrying a simple message calculated to space and time universal. Many visitors to the Grand Canyon are disappointed. The place is too predictable. It is a constant repetition of itself. Once the overall scheme is conceptualized, many visitors find nothing else to see.

overly balanced in its parts, and it epitomizes harmony. As Bloomer and Moore note, the grid is a powerful ambiguous system, at once authoritative (it can be imposed onto a piece of the earth's surface the designer has never even seen) and democratic (the pieces, within some bounds, are interchangeable and negotiable). It is orderly, very easy to describe, and, hence, altogether unmemorable. Nairn criticizes the indistinguishable blocks that decimate the variety available. He calls such landscapes "strip with no tease." There is little sense of discovery and little possibility for continuous spatial experience. There is no "come-on."[16]

Cosmic landscapes are infinite extensions of monotonous plain embraced by encircling vaults of sky. For Norberg-Schultz the desert landscapes of North Africa typify the concept. He writes: "As a whole, the environment seems to make an absolute and eternal order manifest, a world which is distinguished by permanence."[17] Similar landscapes in the American Southwest appear infinite in their monotony, distinguished by absolute order. The Grand Canyon, for example, can be easily understood as an integrated logical system, and seems rational and abstract in the sense of transcending individuality (fig. 4.19). Such landscapes suggest necessity rather than expression. They are simple, balanced, and harmonious to the extreme. They want for visual surprise and mystery. They are too easily known. Such landscapes do not seem to contain individual places, but form merely a continuous neutral ground. *Infinity* is a word that characterizes such places. Infinity implies a "foreverness" because attention is forever focused on an ever-receding horizon. Seeing in detail is little rewarded in the face of such intense predictability. The broad scale of comprehension dominates all.

Whether romantic, classical, or cosmic landscapes actually exist is not at issue here. These categories are useful, however, as they demonstrate how sightseers might assess the appropriateness of detail in a visual array. They represent possible mental templates whereby the aptness of things becomes part of the character of a place perceived. It is a recognition that in the syntax of landscape visual events can have some internal balance or unity. It is an awareness that the relationships among things are more important than the things themselves.

Rhyme and Rhythm

Sense of appropriateness is enhanced by rhyme and rhythm in landscape. Their nature and interrelation help define landscape in romantic, classical, or cosmic terms. Rhyme involves recurring correspondences that bind or tie. They are likenesses that offer special relationship. Peter Smith identifies three types of rhyme: iconic, dimensional coordination, and metaphoric.[18] Iconic rhyme, the most important visually, involves repetition echoing from feature to feature. Within the context of a building facade or within an entire street of buildings some features are seen to repeat in combination through inflection. It is the continuation of cornice line relative to roof, the level of window relative to ground, and the repetition of window bay relative to flat lower facade that seems to tie otherwise diverse buildings together along the San Francisco street pictured in figure 4.20. Dimensional coordination rhyme binds forms of like dimension or scale. A telephoto lens compresses terrace houses in Bath, England, to emphasize their similarity of scale (fig. 4.21). Form reflected in overall bulk echoes down the street, each house representing in broad outlines the very image of its neighbors. Metaphoric rhyme involves only subtle echoes or hints in decoration. Relationship derives neither through the repetition of numerous components nor through the repetition of basic form, but from the suggestion of sameness in difference. Selected components are different, but

Figure 4.20
Iconic rhyme—San Francisco, California. The correspondences of window size and shape, thrust of bay, and overhang of eaves and cornice persist as these dwellings elbow one another in stair-step fashion down the hill toward San Francisco Bay. Each building is different, but, nonetheless, is also tied to neighbors through echoed similarities.

Figure 4.21
Dimensional coordination rhyme—Bath, England. Houses of equal dimension crowd down this street in Bath. Although each stands separately on its lot, the sense of visual coalescence produces an integrated block or terrace.

enough alike to suggest a bond. The arches pictured at London's Covent Garden illustrate this (fig. 4.22). They echo both design and functional relationship.

Rhythm in landscape has been variously defined. Smith differentiates between serial and binary rhythm. Serial rhythm is comparatively simple as a straightforward repeating of objects or object relationships in metered cadence. It evokes, according to Smith, deep-seated satisfaction, a limbic response. Such rhythm is very obvious on New York City's

Figure 4.22

Metaphoric rhyme—London's
Covent Garden. Different classes
of arch maintain correspondence,
speaking of one another
metaphorically.

Sixth Avenue in the panels of the Rockefeller Center office
towers pictured in figure 4.23. Although such cadence is
evident in the San Francisco and Bath scenes already presented,
here binary rhythm is strident, a dominant visual character that
seizes the eye and holds it. Within each building, panel follows
panel. Along the street, building follows building. Binary
rhythm, on the other hand, involves a dialectic between opposites in the sequence of repetition: height/depth, constriction/
openness, or darkness/light. It evokes a more intellectual
response. At the San Diego yacht basic shown, hulls and spars
and masts and mooring posts play off against one another in
repetitive juxtaposition (fig. 4.24). Niels Prak, on the other
hand, defines three kinds of rhythm: regular, variable, and
irregular.[19] All three play across the facades of New York
City's Astor Place (fig. 4.25). Regular rhythms are easily
predicted as sequences inviolate. Variable rhythms either
increase or decrease the cadence in a regulated manner whereas

Figure 4.23

Serial rhythm—New York City's Sixth Avenue. Office buildings march up the avenue in steady cadence: a series of massive visual events reduced to the redundancy of individual vertical panels. It is this redundancy that visually binds the street together.

Figure 4.24

Binary rhythm—yacht basin at San Diego, California. Rhythms in the horizontal (hulls and spars) and the vertical (masts and mooring posts) operate in playful opposition.

irregular rhythms are intermittent and variously metered. Regular rhythms evoke a sense of movement in landscape as an observer anticipates redundancies ahead. Increasing rhythm heightens this impression; decreasing rhythm lessens it. Irregular rhythm, on the other hand, lacks steady cadence and only suggests redundancy. Irregular rhythm enhances romanticism in landscape where dimensional and metaphoric rhymes predominate. Classicism in landscape results from regular and variable rhythms where iconic rhyme predominates. Cosmic landscapes are like classical landscapes

Figure 4.25

Regular, variable, and irregular
rhythms—New York City's
Astor Place. All three types of
rhythm reverberate across the
facades of these buildings. Within
each section of each structure
(base, shaft, and capital by
analogy to the classical column)
elements repeat in regular
cadence. But within the facade of
each structure sections are played
off one another forming either
variable or irregular cadences.

except that the elements rhymed are minimal and the rhythms
fewer.

Rhythms can play against one another to enforce an overall
sense of landscape character. To illustrate, I include a photograph of one of the most widely discussed landscapes in the
United States, the Las Vegas Strip (fig. 4.26). Architects
Robert Venturi, Denise Brown, and Steven Izenour view
Las Vegas as an archetypal classical landscape. It is a city made
comprehensible through the discovery of rhythms. The Strip
in Las Vegas, they assert, reads only as chaos if the observer
perceives only architectural forms. Landscape order lies in the
redundancy and cadence of various landscape rhythms and the
manner by which they rhyme. Thus they write:

> The continuous highway itself and its systems for turning are
> absolutely consistent. The median strip accommodates the
> U-turns necessary to a vehicular promenade for casino crawlers
> as well as left turns onto the local street pattern which the Strip
> intersects. The curbing allows frequent right turns for casinos
> and other commercial enterprises and eases the difficult transi-
> tions from highway to parking. The streetlights function
> superfluously along many parts of the Strip which are inciden-
> tally but abundantly lit by signs; but their consistency of form
> and position and their arching shapes begin to identify by day
> a continuous space of the highway, and the constant rhythm

Figure 4.26

Multiple rhythms—the Strip, Las Vegas, Nevada. Various rhythms pulse along the street: signs marking the large casinos, light standards, turning lanes, driveways, parking lots. These rhythms are more apparent to the motorist than to the pedestrian. Motorists cover distance rapidly, seeing more of the street in a given period of time. Las Vegas is a new automobile landscape that almost requires an automobile to comprehend.

contrasts effectively with the uneven rhythms of the signs behind.

This counterpoint, they emphasize, reinforces the contrast between two types of order on the Strip: the obvious visual order of street elements, and the difficult visual order of buildings and signs.[20]

Openings as Gaps

Things produce rhythms at various scales. However, openings and open spaces may also display rhythmic associations. The sequencing of open spaces in a city may set up patterns of alternating enclosure and open expansiveness. Openings in a building facade may suggest rhythmic penetration. Indeed, openness in a landscape, especially townscapes, may depend on rhythmic relationships for visual effectiveness. As Nairn argues, a gap must mean something in a sequence of visualization or the experience will break down. Rudolf Arnheim suggests that a space must relate, not only to other spaces, but also to surrounding solids in a rhyme of openness and solidity. Spaces need to appear pervaded by perceptual forces or what Arnheim calls "visual substance."[21]

Emptiness is not simply the absence of matter. It is as well the absence of relationship. Emptiness produces gaps in landscape and these gaps, rather than forming rhythms or

completing rhymes, serve to disrupt. Any kind of landscape
can suffer from emptiness. A gap in a romantic setting may
reduce the sense of anticipation as the mystery is disclosed and
surprise eliminated. A gap in a classical landscape may bring
imbalance and discord as overall patterns are disrupted. Gaps
usually result when elements are removed and not replaced in
visual kind, as illustrated in downtown Dallas (fig. 4.27).
However, gaps also result from improper land division or
from some other aspect of land management where useless
slots of space remain. Grady Clay refers to "fragging": the
fragmentation of landscape as pictured in St. Louis
(fig. 4.28).[22] Strands in the fabric of a place seem to have been
eliminated and not replaced, the loose ends left to dangle.

Street furniture and vegetation, among other objects of
place, can be used to obscure gaps in a street scene. Pavements
can be patterned in empty spaces to suggest visual substance.
Such visual detail can be used to enhance the established

Figure 4.28

Fragging—St. Louis, Missouri. Empty fragments of land remain where this new freeway cuts across the grain of the traditional street grid. Such fragments, too small to develop, remain visually derelict. Lost is a sense of cohesion in landscape.

rhythms of a place. Or new rhythms can be set up amongst the various categories of detail to offer additional visual message. From a search for such patterns comes a sense that some things fit and others do not. Those things that fit dominate the pleasurable seeing of place as scenery, whereas those things that do not fit set up negative tensions seen to detract.

FACE

Seeing in detail has still another important dimension: the search for a human quality in place, which Robert Campbell calls "face." Face, as an element of landscape, resides in the facades of buildings as they stand singly or in combination. Traditional buildings in which windows are punched through solid walls appear almost humanoid to Campbell. Such windows, like human eyes, imply "intelligences behind them looking out" (fig. 4.29). Such facades make the city appear social and thus alive. Windows express not only the spatial structure of the individual building, but also the way it is related to light. The glass of modern buildings is light reflecting by day, but light generating by night. The mask of solid surface is lowered to expose internal enclave and the viewer is able to penetrate the face of the city. It is primarily in windows, Norberg-Schultz argues, that the *genius loci* of a place is focused and explained.[23]

Figure 4.29

Face—Toronto, Ontario.

Toronto's city hall seems to peek

from behind an encompassing

cloak. Windows, like human

eyes, imply intelligence, giving

"face" to a landscape.

Face, as a visual element of landscape, derives from the nature of facades as windowed spaces and from the viewer's orientation. Most vistas excite oblique views of facades because facades are seen peripherally in movement. Only with terminated and deflected vistas or in enclosures is the viewer inclined to confront facades. Arnheim notes that such frontality establishes a firm eye contact. A building looks one straight in the face with an almost aggressive initiate. Confrontation is head on. "As a rule," Arnheim writes, "an obliquely placed person sees himself as being out of step with the spatial framework of the place, not the place as facing him obliquely."[24] Frontality places emphasis on primary as opposed to secondary profiles. A primary profile is the outline of a building's front elevation seen head on, as pictured from an Ohio main street (fig. 4.30). A secondary profile is created by the protruding signs and other ephemera which extend outward from a building to counteract the difficulties of oblique viewing, as pictured in a New Brunswick town (fig. 4.31).

Figure 4.30
Primary profiles—Main Street,
Greenville, Ohio. When a facade
is seen in full frontal view, it is
said to display its primary profile.
Primary profiles strike the
strongest silhouettes to attract
and hold the eye. Places designed
to be approached and viewed
from a set location usually present
a primary profile toward that
position.

Figure 4.31
Secondary profiles—Main Street,
St. Andrews, New Brunswick.
When a facade is seen obliquely it
displays its secondary profile.
Secondary profiles are often
dominated by signs hung at the
perpendicular to catch the eyes of
passersby.

The visual power of a primary profile varies with the angle at
which the sightseer confronts a facade's elevation. When the
sightseer approaches a building, it appears to "loom" before
him, "looming" being the magnification of the visual angle of
an object that produces an apparent size transformation. As the
viewer draws closer to a building from a relatively distant
point, Higuchi notes, the building gradually emerges from its
background and begins to create a "purely pictorial" impression. It first begins to take on monumental characteristics
when its angle reaches 18 degrees. When this angle increases to

27 degrees, the building fills the range of vision, and the eye sees the large details. Eventually, when the viewer reaches a point where the angle is 45 degrees, he is at the best place for observing the comparatively small details.[25]

At the scale of the street, complex face tends to retard eye movement and slow the sense of momentum implicit in a vista. An absence of openings suggests exclusion and the eye and the body is encouraged onward. Many openings, especially where they create a vertical rhythm, provide a counterforce to movement. Horizontal organization tends to be directed or movement oriented, whereas vertical organization, which draws the eye up, counter to horizontal movement, is more static. The openings of building facades not only establish visual and functional linkages between interior and exterior domains, but also, through their design, acknowledge and reinforce the special role of the public sector fronted upon.[26] A complex face enhances the public space by inviting pause. Where complexity involves elaborate secondary profiles the impulse to pause is heightened. Signs, especially, draw the eye to amplify the sense of enclave implicit in building entrances.

Texture is an important aspect of face. Texture is determined by the arrangement and size of parts. The concept may apply at various scales from that of total landscape to that of building facades. Texture is a function of alternating solid and transparent surfaces. It is also a function of the material substances that comprise these surfaces. Texture has to do with the tempo of rhythm set up among the elements of a facade so that a surface appears variously grained from fine to coarse. Rhythmically textured facades along a street show smooth faces from a distance and propel the eye forward as the angle of view becomes increasingly oblique. In the view of London's Regent's Park Circle, facade repetitions coalesce when viewed at an oblique angle reducing the sense of texture (fig. 4.32). Coarsely textured facades along a street tend to arrest the eye. Below the scale of the building facade, the term *texture* applies equally well to the grain of specific building materials used in construction, especially as various textures are seen to reflect light differently.

Figure 4.32

Texture in architecture—
Regent's Park Circle in London.
Here is a heavily textured facade
full of shadow-rendering
indentions. When viewed at the
oblique, however, the repetition
of columns and windows carries
the eye rapidly forward,
generalizing and smoothing the
whole. Texture is thus a function
of the viewing angle as well as a
function of the light reflective
properties of architecture.

LIGHT

Light is the primary medium through which most people
perceive and experience the world. Spatial experience,
Gyorgy Kepes notes, is intimately connected with the experience of light. "Without light there is no vision, and without
vision there can be no visible space. Space in a visual sense is
light-space."[27] Light varies according to whether its source is
sunlight or artificial. Each kind of light gives its own special
effect in illuminating the surfaces of objects. Light perceived
directly from the sun, fire, or electrical filament differs substantially from light modulated from these sources in reflection. Reflected light dominates man's seeing. Thus the angle of
light cast upon a surface influences the visual character of a
thing as its nature as a three-dimensional form shows in the
shadows cast (fig. 4.33). Objects do not receive uniform
illumination from every angle. The surface of a sphere, a cube,
or any other form gives its own characteristic distribution of
light. Spherical surfaces, for example, reflect light with sudden
contrasts of light and dark values. The length, shape, and
brightness of a cast shadow gives information about form as it
also indicates the extent and shape of gaps between solids.[28]

Color conveyed by light is a most important detail of place
character. A bright color scheme may express gaiety and
excitement as opposed to the sense of dignity and repose ex-

Figure 4.33

Light as shadow—New York City. The forms of objects show in shadows cast, cueing much not seen directly.

pressed by a quiet scheme. A uniform color scheme may contribute a sense of unity whereas a varied scheme may give a feeling of diversity. Color may express the nature of materials by amplifying a sense of texture. Color may define form as objects (or parts of objects) are contrasted with their surroundings. Color may affect a sense of proportion; materials with contrasting colors laid in horizontal lines tend to emphasize breadth, and vertical lines tend to promote a sense of height. Color imparts scale when elements of a building or adjacent buildings are of contrasting colors. Finally, color gives a sense of weight. Dark elements appear heavy whereas light elements look light in weight.[29]

Color is measured according to hue, brightness, and saturation. Hue is that attribute by which one color can be differentiated from another with red, yellow, and blue the elementary shades or tints that human eyes can distinguish, other colors, such as orange and purple, being mixtures of these primary hues. Measurement is usually based on the arrangement of the colors on a wheel and, in an analogy to the compass, a color's hue is termed its direction. Brightness or value, on the other hand, refers to the extent of difference between a given color and black, as the darkest value, and white, as the lightest. Brightness depends on the proportion of light reflected by a surface. Finally, color saturation or purity is the apparent vividness or chroma. The more pigment carried by a medium the stronger, darker, or more saturated the color becomes.[30] Colors rarely stand alone and the hue, brightness, and saturation of a given surface is modified by adjacent surfaces. Thus if red and green objects are juxtaposed, the red appears redder than if viewed in a background of closer hue. Colors that contrast most strongly lie opposite each other on the color wheel.[31]

Color is not something easily intellectualized because it plays more on the emotions than on the intellect. Words convey color comprehensions with great difficulty. Photographer John Hedgecoe writes: "The vocabulary we normally use in describing colors rarely rises much above the level of 'the sky is blue, the grass is green.' The color labels of a child's paint box are likely to defeat us. How many people can confidently match such closely related terms as umber and ochre, or chrome and saffron or cobalt and indigo, with the colors they name?"[32]

Color is a dictator of mood. Mood can be established by a single color and by colors in combination, both as they contrast and as they harmonize. Reddish hues are often described as warm, bluish ones as cold. Focal length is longer for reds and yellows than for blues and greens and when we look at these colors together, tiny muscular adjustments constantly take place in the eye to cope with wavelength differences. Large areas of contrasting color jostling each other in a scene, Hedgecoe notes, create a "restless duality" of interest, and tend to flatten out space to create pure pattern. Mood also can be established by color harmony, but it is a gentler mood with more subtle pleasures. Harmonic colors are grouped closely together on the color wheel and make up only a restricted palette, consisting usually of two colors in desaturated hues. Reddish colors seem to advance toward the viewer, while blue seems to recede. Paul Spreiregen notes that dark objects seen against light backgrounds recede, while light objects seen against dark backgrounds advance visually. Warm-hued buildings also advance, whereas cool-hued buildings recede and seem less solid.[33]

A color mood can invite action or inaction. With bright illumination and warm and luminous colors (for example, yellow or pink) the mind is directed outward. Such an environment, psychologist Faber Birrens maintains, is conducive to "muscular effort, action, and cheerful spirit." With softer surroundings, cooler hues (for example, blue and green), and lower brightness there is less distraction and a person is better able to concentrate on difficult mental tasks. Motor activity is reduced. Shadows can influence a person's color sense because even intense colors lose their brilliance in subdued light. Color changes with the diurnal cycle. Facades that face east receive a bright morning sunlight; those that face west receive a more subdued, even light. North elevations receive the least light of all, and are therefore most effective when painted a light color; south elevations, by contrast, can take strong and brilliant colors best of all. Under conditions of bright, clear sunlight, the individual parts of buildings stand out, but as light diminishes in the evening or on dull cloudy days the entire composition presents itself to view. Spreiregen notes that vigorously sculptured objects are best seen in even light such as shadow light or northern light, their delicate outlines requiring less light contrast. Thus southern facades may be vigorously articulated whereas northern facades may be more successful if delicately articulated.[34]

Atmospheric change profoundly influences light availability and color effect. Landscapes may be seen in different lights which define different degrees of clarity at different times. Buildings that appear sharply edged in bright sunlight may appear softly edged in a shroud of fog (fig. 4.34). An overcast of cloud distorts sunlight through innumerable reflections and refractions. Distant objects are veiled through a visual weakening of color intensity given the scattering of light by the moisture-laden dust particles suspended in air. The outlines of objects are softened, eliminating detail and giving a sense of depth to a scene. A place may seem to be dominated by a prevailing light condition. Architects Martina Duttmann, Friedrich Schmuck, and Johannes Uhl ask about the city of Paris: "Is the translucent mist of Paris . . . merely a physical phenomenon caused by humidity and pollution or is it more a mood, a collective experience and passion, the scintillating impressionist air that has always hovered like a live thing, over the Seine?"[35] Certainly, quality of atmosphere can give atmosphere or character to place through the associations people are inclined to make.

Light conditions influence legibility of landscape. Legibility,

Figure 4.34

Light and atmosphere—Chicago, Illinois. Evening fog obscures and softens the angularity of the city's skyscrapers to produce a sense of intimacy. Modulated light changes the mood of a landscape. A sense of romance is instilled by that which can only be partially seen.

the capability with which a figure or shape can be recognized against its background, depends on appropriate illumination, the size and shape of the object, and the color contrast between the figure and its background. Light–dark contrast is more important than chromatic contrast. In strong illumination light colors on dark backgrounds are superior; in dim illumination the light background is essential with dark characters clearly contrasted on it. Under bright light space is readily defined, distance can be easily determined, forms appear three-dimensional, while details, colors, and color variations are all clearly seen. When light grows dim, however, space seems to contract, distances cannot be effectively judged, forms tend to flatten out into silhouettes, details are lost, and colors and color values appear to undergo radical change.[36]

At the scale of the individual building, contrasts in light and dark through use of different colors is central to architectural design. According to Martina Duttmann and her associates, color differences usually follow a building's basic division: the foundation or base that connects the building to earth or pavement, the middle zone dominated by windows, and the roof that terminates the building and sets its silhouette against the sky. The finer articulation of a building consists of its relief: elements such as cornices, window frames, niches, projecting bays, balconies, and corner mouldings. Because this relief layer lies before the actual wall of the facade, they term its color

Figure 4.35

Color and disunity—Ledbury, England. color can be used to fragment a building's facade into countless segments, thus breaking up its composition.

"foreground color" to differentiate it from that of the wall itself, which they term "background color." The three zones of a building and its decorative articulation make up an often intricate pattern of planes and projections. Color may be used to emphasize this pattern or to blur it. It can pull a building's zones into one surface or split them into countless fragments by overemphasizing relief.[37] Thus color is used on the English half-timbered house pictured to fragment the facade into its constituent parts (fig. 4.35).

At the scale of the street, color is capable of uniting a row of diverse facades. In the English village shown, color is used to pull individual structures into a coherent ensemble (fig. 4.36). It can also dissolve an architectonically unified street into separate parts. When foregound and background colors alternate from building to building, the space of the street breaks up, rendering the street ambiguous. This break up of space seems to be the predominant role of color in North American cities. Geographer Kenneth Foote's study of building facades in Chicago establishes that buildings tend to be colored in relation to use and the status of the organizations they house. He sees color as permeating Americans' experiencing of cities down to the point where almost every building is differentiated from its neighbor on the basis of change in color, building to building.[38]

Color never acts alone. Differences in building material, for

Figure 4.36

Color as a unifier—Lanreath, Cornwall. Color can be used to unify building facades and to tie structures together as cohesive landscape. Here the white of plastered walls seems to flow from building to building.

example, function with color to either dissolve or unify a street. Where glass, even colored glass, dominates a facade or, indeed, an entire street of facades, color may be very complicated in its relationship to material (fig. 4.37). As Duttmann, Schmuck, and Uhl note, reflections falsify; they alter the proportions of a place and turn directions end for end. They argue that glass walls metamorphose through three stages. Opaque and solid from a distance (and clearly colored), they begin to mirror what is opposite (including the color of opposing facades) as the viewer moves closer. Finally, when the viewer stands directly before them they grow transparent and reveal what is inside (including interior colors). Color, often in very complicated sets of reflections, remains an integral aspect of glassed-in places. As Duttmann and her associates see Paris in shades of gray, they see New York City shimmering in blue: the blue generated by the light of glass-sheathed buildings reflecting one another as they tower above the city's streets.[39]

Nothing influences the light effect of landscape so much as the condition of the sky. Nothing is so much a part of landscape as the constantly varying sky. It provides a sense of horizon and silhouette and otherwise forms a ceiling to one's views. The sky appears as large as the space from which it is seen. Thus in a flat topography largely devoid of trees and

buildings the sky forms a domineering dome encircling the
viewer with distant horizons as in that Kansas panorama
previously pictured (see fig. 3.1). Cloud and other aspects of
atmosphere are seen to comprise much of the scenery, even
when the view is oriented across the land, as in the South
Dakota highway scene with its distant small town
(see fig. 3.38). In confined urban places, by contrast, the walls
of buildings define the sky which is relegated to less importance. Instead of being a comprehensive hemisphere within a
linear horizon, the sky is reduced to background defining the
edges of building contours.[40]

The "visual field" that buildings exert on open spaces is not
only exerted in the horizontal dimension, but also in the vertical direction. The sky not only forms a ceiling, but also forms
a ceiling of apparent height. The subjective impression of a
definite sky-ceiling is produced by the interplay of surrounding building height and the extent of open space surrounded
as illustrated at the principal downtown intersection in

Figure 4.38
The sky confined—Birmingham, Alabama. The sky is reduced to mere background in the city. Among tall buildings the sky seems to provide a ceiling for confined urban spaces.

Birmingham, Alabama (fig. 4.38). Generally, the height above a square or other enclosure is imagined as three or four times the height of the tallest building. The effect is most apparent in small, well-enclosed squares, for as size of space increases and solidity of walls decreases, the surrounding masses appear to exert less influence and a sense of ceiling height becomes increasingly vague. Cloud condition may also give a sense of ceiling height, as for example the "sky dado": a horizontal vista formed by a layer of bright, clear sky between a horizon and a cloud canopy.[41]

CHANGE

The sense of passage, past, present, and future, adds to the character of landscape. Places may be seen as events, as happenings, unwinding in landscape. Places change and places are variously animated. Sightseers have two kinds of evidence suggesting passage of time. Lynch in his classic book *What Time Is This Place?* identifies them as episodic repetition (the heartbeat, breathing, sleeping and waking, hunger, cycles of sun and moon, the seasons, waves, tides, clocks) and progressive and irreversible change (growth and decay).[42] Both combine to enliven landscape through overt physical movement or covert signs of movement. They combine as a collage of timeliness instilling in the sightseer a feeling of here and

Figures 4.39 and 4.40
Diurnal change—Kintbury,
England, and Quebec City. Daily
cycles play off against church
walls in endless rounds of
shadow. Qualities of light and
shadow provide constant cue to
time's passage.

now. Such evidence points to a past, anchors a present, and suggests a future to give meaning to surroundings. The sight-seer inserts himself into the scene as part of that reality, as part of that place in time.

The diurnal and seasonal cycles are the most profound episodic repetitions observed. During the day the surfaces of buildings catch light and change visibly as the sun's angle shifts (figs. 4.39 and 4.40). At night buildings are bathed in artificial light or generate their own illumination through windows lit according to the cycles of life within. Vegetation transforms itself with the seasons and shortening or lengthening of days. Lynch writes of deciduous trees: "Their summer and winter forms are different yet logically and visually connected. Each form stands for a whole cluster of emotional meanings. Between them there are relatively rapid and striking transitions from one episodic phase to another: the unique qualities of contrasting episodes caught in temporal if not

spatial juxtaposition." The sightseer of subtle mind may
delight in reading the time of day or year in nature and may see
therein analogies to many aspects of human life.[43]

Landscapes variously pulse with human activities, affording
each time of day, week, or season its distinctive temporal
rhythms. Cycles of activity and quiet reflect in changing
densities of people. At Boston's Quincy Market a noontime
crowd on a summer's day surges through the plaza, the bustle
of activity substantially defining the place (fig. 4.41). Visible
activity can be characterized by type and by the mix of distinct
types of actions. There are visible flows of people as well as
localized eddies of activity. Lynch writes: "One may concentrate on the movement of people and look for things that
influence that movement: the behavior at decision points, the
barriers and the attractants, the origins and destinations, the
involuntary delays and detours, the way-finding behavior, the
maintenance of personal space while moving, movement,

Figure 4.41
People and diurnal cycles—
Boston, Massachusetts. People
animate places. Here crowds
press the Quincy Market at noon.
The market witnesses an ebb and
flow of customers with the
passing hours. People and their
activities give witness to daily
regimes. Survivals of the past are
manifest in the market today. Old
buildings recycled to current uses
speak of historical change.

conflict, and so forth." Varying forms of territoriality define
character in landscape. Important also are the traces of past
activity.[44] A rural path in England's Cotswolds not only
reflects a place very different from Quincy Market, but a different kind of time as well, a time of quietude. Human activity
can only be implied from signs of passage (fig. 4.42).

Progressive and irreversible change reflects itself in traces
ingrained in the material environment: the worn steps on a
stair, the patina of rust on a porch railing, the collapse of a
garden wall. Such details give a heightened sense of flow of
time. Ruined structures in the process of going back to the
earth, Lynch muses, are enjoyed everywhere for the emotional
sensations they convey. "There is a pleasure in seeing receding,
half-veiled space or in detecting the various layers of successive
occupation as they fade into the past, and then finding a few
fragments whose origins are remote and inscrutable, whose
meanings lurk beneath their shapes, like dim fish in deep
water."[45] The visible relics of past events, as they have
accumulated in overlapping accretions, make apparent the
depth of historical time.

The sightseer's broad outlines of landscape are enriched by
environmental details seen to imbue character to place.
Awareness of scale, sense of appropriateness, search for face,

Figure 4.42

Diurnal cycle—Broadway, England. A path beaten along the edge of this field reflects a public access. Here people in passing have left their mark: a statement about both past and future place intentions.

concern with light, and concern for change complete the macroview variously comprised of panoramas, vistas, focal points, enclosures, enclaves, and points of pause. The sightseer uses both the details and the broad dimensions of his surroundings to compose scenery. In the next chapter I consider landscape as pictures. I will argue that sightseeing is largely a search for the picturesque. Thus I focus not on what the sightseer sees, but on what the sightseer might be inclined to see.

Chapter 5

Landscape as Visual Composition

Scenery exists in the interaction between material reality and human observers.

KENNETH CRAIK

Through first-hand observation in pleasurable surroundings, tourists explore the complexities of the world beyond their everyday existence. Tourism is a significant means by which modern people assess their world, defining a sense of personal identity in the process. Touring involves the logistics of moving, eating, and sleeping, and of purchasing souvenirs—trophies of the travel experience. But beyond such logistics are the experiences themselves that justify touring as the expenditure of time, energy, emotion, and money. The tourist focuses attention on contrived attractions: touring a factory, hiking in a park, visiting a historic site, browsing through an art museum. Watching or looking from controlled vantage points comprises the essence of such experiencing (fig. 5.1).

Again, the kind of sightseeing emphasized in this book concerns not the contrived attractions of tourism so much as the landscapes seen in moving from one specific attraction to another. Pictured in Quebec City's Lower Town. Visitors

116

Figure 5.1
Tourist attraction—Grand Canyon National Park, Arizona. Contrived tourist attractions are designed to be viewed from controlled vantage points. Cameras dominate visual experiencing when tourists seek to replicate popular photographic views of a place. A walkway like the one pictured not only facilitates viewing but also largely determines what it is that is actually seen. The place is contrived as scenery predicated on a set vista, a limited sense of refuge, and an imposed scale of detail.

wander the narrow streets taking in the sights, searching out known attractions, and discovering the unexpected (fig. 5.2). Visualization dissolves into pleasure seeking. It is the often mindless processing of visual imagery as pleasure-giving stimulus. It is the search for scenery to fulfill the tourist's quest for attractive places implying novelty of experience, especially pleasurable novelty. Such visualization requires little verbalization; indeed, much of the pleasure comes from not having to verbalize thoughts at all. Such experience involves "sight-thinking" and not "word-thinking."

The concept of "sight-thinking" comes from John Kouwenhoven, a literary critic and historian. Kouwenhoven notes the ease with which verbal concepts can be recorded and repeated. The power of spoken and written language underlies our whole educational system if not our entire society, he argues. But we must not permit our admiration for "word-thinking" or our dependence on its achievements to bind us to its limitations: shortcomings that derive from the inescapable limitations of words themselves—that is, their "averaging out" tendency. Words reduce experience into categories and in the process of this categorization information is lost. Sight-thinking (as, indeed, the other forms of sensory thought: feel-thought, smell-thought, taste-thought, and sound-thought) does not categorize. It remains the essence of experience without abstraction.[1] It is at this phenomenological level of knowing that sightseeing produces its pleasure.

Figure 5.2

Spontaneous sightseeing—
Quebec City, Quebec. Tourists
amble through the narrow streets
of Lower Town in search of
specific attractions, for example
the excursion boat seen in the
distance. Their sightseeing is
spontaneous as they wander.
They randomly take in sights.
The seeing of this place is not
programmed through the
structured contrivance of any one
attraction except the structuring
of the city itself.

A sight-thought is evanescent. It flashes on one's consciousness, then fades. It is also comprehensive, including all visible
aspects of a thing or place at one and the same instant, whereas
a word-thought has to be accumulated gradually by adding
words together. Most important, Kouwenhoven argues, the
sight-thought is specific, not generalized. People can sight-
think a building or a group of buildings, but they cannot
sight-think the generalized concept of building. Obviously,
sight-thoughts have significant limitations if compared to
word-thoughts. They cannot be arranged in logical or syntac-
tical patterns. Awareness derived cannot be communicated
symbolically without interrupting or even destroying the
sight-thought process itself. Thus sensory awareness cannot be
recorded and reproduced in identical copy. Sight-thoughts are
highly personal.[2]

My purpose is not to champion sensory-thinking, but to
suggest that more can be done to bridge the gap between
sensory experience and verbalization. Martina Duttmann
writes: "There is no School of Seeing. Though we often
remember words, sentences, verses, fragments of prose, and
use them in our speech every day, most people never use what
they see; if they remember it at all, it is only unconsciously, and
they certainly would be hard put to describe what they have
seen."[3] Sensory-thinking has meaning only insofar as people
are able to translate into categorizations a sense of shared
experience. Refining word usage and, indeed, even inventing

Figure 5.3
Seeking perspective—
Hutchinson, Kansas. This grain
elevator seems to disappear
toward a vanishing point. Its
representation in this picture
retains the sense of distance, size,
and relative position that would
be recorded by the unaided eye.
Such three-dimensional
representation has been the
essence of perspectivist art since
the Renaissance. As human
visualization has influenced art,
art has influenced visualization to
the extent that such views are
sought out as pictorially
significant landscape.

new words seems a desirable task. Again, I will content myself
with using established language to sketch the outlines of what
sight-thinking is all about, and to suggest what aspects of
sight-thinking deserve close attention. Pictorial composition,
I believe, is a most important consideration. Through
composition the visual elements of landscape are linked, the
linkage being a kind of unspoken knowing.

COMPOSITION

Composition is manifest in the mental relationships a person
establishes between the visual elements of landscape. To be
noticed a scene must stand out from its context, suddenly
recommending itself as somehow elegant. Each culture, each
society, has set preferences for composing the built environment as visual display. Members of a given society share ways
of composing scenery as conditioned ways of viewing. The
perspectivist tradition of conceptualizing three-dimensional
space in two-dimensional drawings may be the most rigidly
conditioned point of view operant in Western culture.[4] Sense
of perspective may be quite explicit, as it is in the photograph
of the Kansas grain elevator shown in figure 5.3. As pictured,
the massive structure recedes toward the horizon as if drawn
on canvas, the eye slipping toward an eventual vanishing
point. Since the Renaissance, Europeans (and now nearly
everyone in the Western-influenced world) have been condi-

tioned to value scenery according to the rules of perspective. Landscape composition, in other words, is as much a function of what people are conditioned to see as it is a function of what exists to be seen.

Perspective, the science by which three-dimensional reality assumes a natural aspect when seen through and recorded on a two-dimensional surface, is but one form of scenic apperception. The rendering of landscape paintings since the Renaissance and the widespread use of photography over the last century and a half have by inculcation influenced greatly what sightseers demand of scenery. Although seldom conscious of what they do, sightseers react favorably to scenes composed like pictures. Unconsciously, sightseers seek in landscape the elements of pictorial composition communicated subliminally in the paintings and photographs they consume. It is important to note that two kinds of composition operate in landscape visualization. There is the composition of the landscape itself as an actual reality of forms variously distributed in space. Of concern here, however, is the manner by which that reality appears to compose itself to the eye. In such comprehension the principles of pictorial composition come to the fore.

Composition in Landscape Painting

Much of the formal development of Renaissance painting, argues art historian Thomas Munro, can be summarized as the gradual achievement of realistic, single-viewpoint perspective: that is, the ability to represent a scene as if perceived as a whole from one point in space at one moment of time under one set of atmospheric lighting conditions. The convergence of parallels toward the horizon and the gradual diminution in size of more and more distant objects, he writes, proceeded in a way that was opposite and complementary to the conewise extension of the vista, reaching out from the imaginary viewpoint: a viewpoint usually located a little above ground to correspond with the eyes of a standing adult in real space. Objects and surfaces seen obliquely were carefully foreshortened and the systematic representation of receding vistas was reinforced by contrasts and alterations of light and dark hue. Other devices included the punctuation of main areas depicted by objects of familiar size and shape to indicate scale, zig-zag recession of continuous lines (such as paths, shadows, shorelines, and building silhouettes) to lead the eye back and forth, and blurring of distant objects as if by mist or heated atmosphere. Such views were unified by light, depicted from a single source, as in a sunset, or by a clearly explained combination of lights, as from windows or lamps. These visual devices also served the painters of the Baroque who carried them to their limits.[5]

In the eighteenth century two masters came to the fore to substantially influence pictorial composition. They created a sense of the ideal in landscape portrayal. Claude Gellée (Claude Lorraine) and Nicolas Poussin masterminded in spacious landscape renderings subtle invitations to imaginary journeys toward far horizons. Claude, historian Kenneth Clark emphasizes, nearly always conformed to a single underlying scheme of composition. It comprised (1) a dark coulisse on one side of the canvas, the shadow of which extended across the foreground; (2) a middle plane or horizon with a large central feature (usually water or a group of trees); and (3) two horizons, one behind the other, the second usually being a luminous distance of cloud. Claude depicted various objects (for example, bridges or cattle fording streams) to lead the eye from one plane to the next, although these were less important than his sense of tone which allowed him to achieve an effect of recession even in pictures where every plane was parallel. Art historian Barbara Novak considers the impact of Claude on American landscape painting as convention become cliché. Trees were made to frame a picture's lateral edges, a dark foreground coulisse led the eye toward a middleground of water, a distant mountain anchored the eye in motifs endlessly permuted.[6]

Poussin conceived that the essence of ideal landscape lay in the harmonious balance of horizontal and vertical elements. Clark writes: "He recognized that the spacing of horizontals and verticals and their rhythmic relation to one another could have an effect exactly like the rhythmic travée or other harmonic devices of architecture; and, in fact, he often disposed them according to the so-called golden section." The difficulty of imposing this geometric scheme on nature lies in an absence of natural verticals. Landscape, especially pastoral landscape, is essentially horizontal, and the verticals that exist are not always at right angles to the ground. Thus Poussin introduced architecture to carry pure geometry right through his compositions. Insistence on the right angle was only possible where the main axis of the composition was parallel to the picture plane, and this, Clark notes, accounted for the frontality of Poussin's landscapes. But since penetration into space was an essential part of landscape painting, Poussin had to devise means of leading the eye back into the distance. Thus he added diagonals that would conduct the eye smoothly and rhythmically to the background. He was particularly fond of a diagonal path that turned back on itself some two-thirds of the distance into the picture.[7]

The nineteenth century brought major innovations, especially the depiction of very transitory momentary configurations suggesting movement rather than permanence and impressionistic coloring that likewise emphasized the evanescent aspect of scenes. To Munro these developments were only partly consistent with the single-vista concept, edging away from it through weakening the definiteness of the imaginary viewpoint. Also these developments tended to diminish the size of the vistas portrayed from the grandly monumental to the casual, small, and intimate. To Clark impressionism created its own consistency of vision: the sensational unity of the glance or snapshot. Clark concludes that the measured interplay of horizontals and verticals, the use of a house, a window, or a block of masonry as a modulus of proportion, the diagonal that turns back on itself, the arc whose ideated center is a nodal point in the composition, all these devices were foreign to the impressionists, and may have seemed irreconcilable with their technique. Thus impressionism would bring to popular landscape appreciation a developed sense of form as light and color, but leave to traditional devices the sense of pictorial composition. That this is true is clearly reflected in most "how to paint" books which today instruct the neophyte in the popular art of constructing landscapes on canvas.[8]

Although "how-to-book" approaches to landscape painting may or may not produce good art, such instruction does convey the character of pictorial composition popularly conceived. Norman Battershill, in his book *Light on the Landscape,* encourages "a firm structure of composition." First position the horizon line, he advises the landscapist, in order to determine the proportions of terrain to sky. Then outline the main masses and principal rhythmic lines, ignoring all minor detail. Next paint in the general tone of the large masses and at the same time indicate the strong areas of shadow. Finally, set the center of interest in the system of receding planes, having established a system of perspective. In other words, the artist should begin by looking for the most important shapes and relate these with one another for proportion and location in the picture. Only then does the artist turn for effect to the detail of color.[9]

Composition in Landscape Photographs

Photography freed painting for abstraction: painting's great twentieth-century vocation. Abstract artists ignore landscape as object reality, and depicting landscape as the eye might see it has fallen primarily to photographers. Similar but decidedly different kinds of landscape imagery have been the result. First, the camera invites a very different artistic orientation to landscape in contrast even to realistic painting. Painters construct whereas photographers disclose. Painters select from the landscape, ignoring much and emphasizing little. They add and rearrange to contrive on canvas scenes suggestive rather than iconic. Photographers have fewer degrees of freedom. They can emphasize or deemphasize according to their selection of viewpoint and focus of lens, but the realities of landscape remain variously fixed on the film. Photographer John Szarkowski writes: "Photography is a system of visual editing. At bottom [it] is a matter of surrounding with a frame a portion of one's cone of vision, while standing in the right place at the right time."[10]

In addition, the camera lens introduces distortion. Susan Sontag notes that photographic seeing is a kind of dissociative seeing, a subjective habit that is reinforced by the objective discrepancies between the way the camera and the human eye focus and judge perspective. Photographic perspective is greatly exaggerated because there is a negligible distance between the lens of the camera, which corresponds to the eye of the observer, and the space or objects seen. In artistic perspective, which is used ordinarily by the painter, a certain amount of distance between the eye and the pictorial aperture is taken into account, and this distance tends to reduce the extreme discrepancies in size between the near and the far in the pictorial depth. The lack of this distancing in photographs was a major concern in the early days of photography and only after people began to see photographically (that is, after the photograph became the standard for depicting landscape) did they stop talking about what was called "photographic distortion."[11]

The language by which photographs are evaluated is meagre and, as Sontag points out, parasitical on the vocabulary of composition in painting. Consider how novice photographers are instructed to compose pictures. John Hedgecoe writes in his book *The Art of Color Photography* that a good composition should lead the eye to a single main subject and then let it explore the rest of the picture. In a picture with depth, the line of movement should run from the foreground through the middle distance to the background. A fundamental principle is that colors, lines, and shapes should be balanced so that they help convey the main statement of the picture instead of causing conflict. He writes: "The classical divisions of space used in painting can be equally effective in photography. If you mentally divide whatever you intend to photograph into thirds, both horizontally and vertically, objects positioned on these divisions, and especially at intersections, are given added emphasis."[12]

The camera invites everyone to play the artist in making pictures. It serves as the final connecting link between the innate ability to see and the external capability to report, interpret, and express what one sees without having to have special talent or extended training to effect the process. Not only have the masses embraced the photograph as a view of reality, but they have also embraced the camera as a means of approaching reality. Donis Dondis writes: "Most of what we know and learn, what we buy and believe, what we recognize and desire, is determined by the domination of the human psyche by the photograph."[13] Thus what we see is a major part of what we know and photographic art greatly influences what we see through conventionalized representation.

Sontag argues persuasively that photographic seeing has altered social consciousness. Photographs alter and enlarge our notions of what is worth looking at and what we have the right to observe. She notes that photographs are a grammar and, even more important, an ethic of seeing. I might observe that in no social context has the camera had greater impact than in tourism. People regularly travel beyond the confines of habitual places and most of them consider it positively unnatural to travel for pleasure without a camera. Photographs offer indisputable evidence that a trip was made, that fun was had. Photographs document sequences of place consumption. However, photography can tyrannize. As photographs are a means of certifying experience, they are also a way of refusing it by limiting it to a search for the photogenic, by converting experience into images as souvenirs. Thus travel often dissolves sightseeing into a quest for pictures. Compulsion to photograph or to see things photographically turns into a way of seeing. Ultimately, according to Sontag, having an experience becomes identical with taking a photograph. She writes: "Taking photographs has set up a chronic voyeuristic relation to the world which levels the meaning of all events."[14]

COMPOSITION AS UNITY

A picture may illustrate people, buildings, trees, lakes, and mountains, but these do not make a picture until they have been arranged or composed. Indeed, without composition there can be no picture because the composition of pictorial elements into a whole is the picture.[15] For the best composition, the parts should be organized so that the whole is seen before the parts. The eye should wander peacefully over the details and not jump back and forth aggressively. Successful composition as underlying structure forms a total configuration, suggesting an immediate and simultaneous presence of all elements. A successful view of landscape has unity like a successful photograph or painting. Dondis writes: "Unity is a proper balance of diverse elements into one totality that is visually all of a piece. The collection of many units should dovetail so completely that it is viewed and considered as a single thing." Unity exists when a picture achieves a network of equalized forces that, no matter how sparse or dense, function throughout the entire configuration. Art historian Donald Weisman writes: "By unity we mean the quality or condition of being one in feeling or purpose. By unity in a work of art we mean that the work affects us as a thing complete in itself: a homogeneous configuration in which elements not only are compatible, but caused to unite in what we sense as an inseparable whole."[16]

Although sightseers rarely experience a sense of complete scenic cohesion, they unknowingly search for composed pictures predicated on their repeated exposure to the rules of composition implicit in the photographs and other art works daily encountered. Of course, good composition is something the eye can be trained to see. Sightseers can rise above unconscious reaction to scenery to levels of conscious recognition. The appreciation of music serves by analogy. Although music is composed and most landscapes are not, the ear of the untrained listener finds much in common with the eye of the untrained observer. Untrained listeners perceive little else but obvious tuneful melodies in symphonic music. More highly trained listeners can focus attention first on the rhythmic variations and then on the orchestration. They can enjoy selective apperception by focusing attention on one component after another. They can listen for counterpoint and polyphonic development in the melodic lines, then for harmony, chord progression and modulations, then for changes in meter and rhythm.[17] So also might sightseers be asked to rise above pure visual impression to ask how landscapes form in the mind's eye as pictures. They should not be left satisfied with superficial seeing. They should be encouraged to see how each component of landscape fits the whole.

Among the many aspects of composition appropriate to landscape appreciation, the following seem to me most important: enframement, balance, focal center, and entrance/exit. Each aspect contributes to the unity of a scene in a different way. Enframement sets a view apart from other views by confining visual attention. Balance gives a sense of stability. Focal center provides attraction to hold the eye, whereas the sense of entrance/exit enables the eye to enter and leave a pictured landscape comfortably. Knowingly or unknowingly, sightseers respond to landscape as compositions when these elements successfully unify a given visual array.

Enframement

For the painter the very act of representing reality inside a frame brings a degree of compositional unity. For the photographer the finite edges of a viewfinder serve the same

Figure 5.4

Enframement—Stanford University, Palo Alto, California. The arch frames a picture leading the eye forward toward another vista soon to be exposed. Here architecture serves, as does the frame for a painted canvas, to aid the sightseer in seeing pictorially.

purpose. Detaching a visual array from its environmental context to surround it with a clear border creates, in and of itself, an internal cohesion. The frame restricts the viewer's attention, thus capturing the eye.[18] The sightseer may or may not confront scenes enframed. For the pedestrian an overarching canopy of trees may define the axis of a vista or the arch of portal may enframe, as is most effectively accomplished at the center of the Stanford University campus shown in figure 5.4. Arches selectively reveal a space to give it special status. By affording formal limits to a panorama, arches elevate the framed view, giving it an "epic" significance. Framing can also bring a distant scene forward by focusing attention and emphasizing detail not otherwise seen.[19] For the motorist, the automobile windshield serves as a framing device. A tunnel portal or an overpass may enhance the framed effect: a frame within a frame.

Balance

Pictorial unity stems from counterbalancing the visual influences of dissimilar objects. Albany's Empire State Plaza is a lesson in counterbalance: its structural components carefully played against one another to form striking views at key points of approach (figs. 5.5 and 5.6). Balance, as displayed in the plaza, refers to equilibrium (equal balance between opposing forces), equipoise (equal distribution of weight), and counterpoise (counterbalancing weight and positions). A work of art

---

Landscape as Visual Composition

Figures 5.5 and 5.6
Balance—Empire State Plaza,
Albany, New York. The
architect directs the visitor's
approach to the plaza presenting
a balanced picture. Balance holds
in both the vertical and horizontal
dimensions.

or an architectural design is in balance to the extent that its
elements and their qualities have been poised against each other
so that they are equalized. The most important psychological
as well as physical influence on human perception, Dondis
observes, is our need for balance. Equilibrium is our firmest
and strongest visual reference, both the conscious and unconscious basis for making judgments. Thus the horizontal-
vertical construct, he argues, is our basic relationship to the
environment. "In visual expression or interpretation, this process of stabilization imposes on all things seen and planned a
vertical 'axis' with a horizontal secondary referent which together establish the structural factors that measure balance."[20]

Equilibrium in pictures may be achieved through bilateral,
asymmetrical, and radial symmetry.[21] Bilateral symmetry
distributes pictorial elements equally about a centered vertical
axis, as in the photograph of Salisbury Cathedral (fig. 5.7).

Exact correspondence of size and position in opposing parts is achieved since one-half of the configuration appears as the mirror image of the other. Asymmetrical balance poses size and position against each other, as in the photograph of Detroit's Renaissance Center (fig. 5.8). Asymmetrical balance may be likened to the placing of unequal weights at different distances from a fulcrum, thus achieving balance. A very important object placed but a short distance on one side of a center point may be balanced by a very small object on the other side of center, but farther removed from it. Radial symmetry employs a center point around which pictorial components are repeated in all directions in corresponding manner as suggested in the vaulted ceiling of Wells Cathedral (fig. 5.9). Symmetry is achieved relative to the horizontal as well as to the vertical.

Of the three kinds of equilibrium, the sense of asymmetrical balance is most important to landscape visualization. Only classical landscapes deliberately designed for symmetry convey absolute balance when viewed frontally. Reflections in water or glass can only suggest radial balance at the landscape scale. In viewing ordinary scenes, the eye is set to balancing the diverse components of landscape as they relate asymmetrically. Every object in landscape has a certain positive power, as though each object were a magnet of given potency. Each has attraction for the eye and each, while drawing attention for

Figure 5.7
Bilateral symmetry—Salisbury
Cathedral, Salisbury, England.
The cathedral's nave is perfectly
balanced. Architectural elements
on the left mirror those on the
right.

Figure 5.8
Asymmetrical balance—
Renaissance Center, Detroit,
Michigan. Here balance is
achieved by playing volume
(dark) and void (light) against a
sense of near and far so that each
comprises approximately half the
view as variously distributed.

Figure 5.9

Radial symmetry—Wells Cathedral, Wells, England. The vault of the cathedral ceiling radiates outward. Such symmetry is restricted to enveloping architectural forms and contributes little to a sense of pictorial composition in landscape.

itself, establishes proportional detraction for every other part. The eye discovers equilibrium as it sorts out the contending forces. Sense of unity lies in the balancing of disparate forces according to the size of objects and their distance from center fulcrum.[22]

Focal Center

Successful pictures, and successful views, contain a worthy center of interest to which all else is subordinated. Part of every scene should attract the eye like a magnet. The focal center may be established by any means of attraction, such as convergence, or by various types of contrast. Accent by convergence occurs when two lines or two planes are seen to come together. Two lines at some distance apart cannot be viewed without the eye moving constantly from one to the other. As the two lines converge, the eye bridges the shortened interval with less effort and, consequently, interest is drawn toward the con-

Figure 5.10

Focal center—Trinity,
Newfoundland. In this scene the
church captures the eye
subordinating the other pictorial
elements around its pivotal point.
In composing mental pictures of
landscape, the eye searches for
such center focus.

vergence that produces a sense of nodality. When several relationships of convergence tend to arrive at one common point,
an inescapable area of attraction is formed.[23]

The focal center of a picture or scene is also the pivot point
around which various contrasting components group themselves, pulling and warring, in their claim for attention. The
church dominates the scene in the Newfoundland fishing
village pictured (fig. 5.10). Houses angle toward it. It
emphasizes the break between land and sea. It appears to be the
pivot point between foreground buildings and distant
mountains.[24] As focal center it is the balance point around
which various correspondences operate. Painters and photographers arrange pictorial components to effectuate "secret
geometries," the lines and planes of which variously converge
to direct the eye to such focal centers. The standard geometric
schemes used include S-shaped curves, triangles, crosses, and
rectangles.[25] In the photograph, open space assumes a
triangular form, taking the church and the lower corners of the
photograph as the angle points. Use of light and shadow and
the portrayal of solid form and open space add up beneath the
obvious portrayal of object reality to focus the eye on a central
core of interest. The sightseer searches for a focal center upon
which to fix the eye. To this center all else seems subordinated
in a unified visual array, balanced if not enframed.

Entrance/Exit

A well-composed picture or scene not only attracts the eye, but helps lead the eye into and out of the composition, thus enhancing the sense of unity. Generally, the eye enters a scene in the foreground and exits at the horizon line. Objects in the foreground should not block the eye diverting its course from plane to plane. In viewing pictures the entering eye of the Westerner usually favors the left-hand and lower portion of the visual field. Dondis emphasizes that there is a scanning pattern in Western society that responds first to a vertical-horizontal referent and then to a left-lower perceptual pull. The tendency to the left may be influenced by Western print formation. Certainly, there is a strong visual conditioning in the way Europeans learn to read from left to right. Thus when visual material conforms to our expectations in terms of the felt vertical axis, the horizontal stabilizing base, the dominance of the left-hand area of the field over the right, and the lower half of the visual field over the upper half, one has, Dondis asserts, a composition of minimal stress. When the opposite conditions obtain, one has maximum stress.[26] As illustrated by the Colorado scene (fig. 5.11), in the successful composition the eye enters where expected, moves readily to the focal center, dwells there assessing detail, and then exits. Visualizing landscape is a continuous sequencing of such compositional determinations. Thus with the Colorado landscape pictured the eye enters toward the lower right. It moves up and across the valley following the diagonals of the creek toward the cleft in the mountains located in the upper center of the picture. The snowcap suggests a source for the stream whose valley the eye surveys. The eye exits the frame at the horizon with subsequent viewing scanning for details not at first seen.

LEGIBILITY

Landscapes, quite obviously, are comprised of objects: streets, buildings, vehicles, people. Objects are grouped visually into landscape configurations. Many objects, and many object groupings, are so large that they are seen over and over again in a person's moving across an area. As dominants in the continuous seeking for pictorial composition, they are highly imageable, defining what planner Kevin Lynch calls "legibility" in landscape. Lynch has developed a general taxonomy to suggest how landscapes are so conceptualized. Lynch, in his book *The Image of the City,* contrasts the business districts of Boston, Jersey City, and Los Angeles. He does not approach landscape from the perspective developed in this book, that is from questions of how people visualize landscape. Rather, having established what people remember of landscapes, he has classified the objects and object clusters noted into broad categories with each category assigned an assumed visual significance. In addition, he does not take the perspective of the sightseer, but that of the commuter as long-time resident.[27]

The sightseer, or any other observer, orients to landscape not through a single view, but through sequences of views or serial vision. Each view influences succeeding views as expectations are built from view to view. The eye is selective in what it sees, predicated on what it is seeing and what it has seen. Objects or clusters of objects that repeat over and over again will be more important to seeing an area than visual isolates for which no pattern of recurrence is evident. These highly legible constructs direct the eye as a given scene is composed. But, more important, these constructs also provide a scaffolding that transcends any individual scene to embrace wider geographical reality. What the sightseer composes as a scene is known to fit into a larger context as scene follows scene. The viewer's image of a city thus adds up to a unified whole based on often repeated referents.[28]

Figure 5.12

Paths—Niagara-on-the-Lake, Ontario. People view landscape in pictorial sequences, the path being followed channeling movement and focusing serial vision along a linear trajectory. Here the path of this highway, a vista enframed and reduplicated by parallel trees, structures a series of views. This place is imageable for the sense of path.

A highly imageable city is structured to facilitate comprehension through serial vision. It contains sufficient legibility to enable the sightseer to gain a sense of totality from the sequenced views of its parts. Even where gaps or other disruptions occur, optical units tend to be shaped into closed compact wholes by the underlying sense of visual organization operating at a macroscale. Visual dominance is the key to legibility. As Lynch notes, clear dominance of one part over others by means of size or intensity results in the viewer reading the whole as an associated cluster. It allows simplification by omission and subsumption. More important, however, is dominance through repetition where components appear over and over in sequenced scenes enabling the piecing together of a larger puzzle, the eye tending to search for those components to the subordination or even exclusion of other components. Dominance through repetition establishes a sense of the relationship through pattern. The components of urban landscape that Lynch sees as forming these legible patterns are: paths, nodes, landmarks, districts, edges.[29]

"Paths" are channels such as sidewalks, streets, and the highways along which people move or potentially move. Pictured is an Ontario highway which provides a clear sense of path: the sense of vista enhanced by trees and light standards (fig. 5.12). Paths are comprised of vistas sequenced as a linear progression following an obvious trajectory of travel. Sightseers see a landscape by moving through it. A good part of

Figure 5.13

Nodes—view from the Empire
State Building, New York City.
Nodes are areas of anticipated
activity into and out of which
people see themselves as
potentially moving. The clusters
of tall buildings in Manhattan's
two business districts (midtown
seen in the foreground and the
financial district seen in the
background) are clear symbols of
geographical convergence.
Nodes are functional entities
given visual force.

their search for the picturesque involves the identification of
pathways. Jay Appleton writes: "In contemplating the pattern
of communications in a landscape the eye tends to fit together
the visible components in such a way as to construct imaginary
paths between its various parts." The mind steers the sightseer,
anticipates what lies ahead, and distinguishes between obstacle
and path. A street, for example, must let the sightseer know
that the path is appropriate. The street must convey a sense of
ready access, of clear direction, and of well-defined boundaries
for safe progress. Streets as paths figure prominently in the
sightseer's attempt to compose pictures in landscape,
especially as streets form ready vistas inviting movement.[30]

"Nodes" are focal points into and out of which people move
as they circulate within an area. They may be enclosures such
as squares or plazas; or they may be enclaves such as bus or railroad terminals. They may be defined at various scales of
comprehension. A city's entire central business district is a
node within the city as it serves as the origin or potential
destination in travel. In the view of Manhattan, two business
district nodes are evident: Midtown in the foreground and the
financial district in the distance (fig. 5.13). Both nodes are
strategic places into which a sightseer can potentially enter.
The high-rise towers of each stand as constant geographical
referents as the sightseer moves around the metropolis.
Whether they really are destinations is not important. They
serve as potential destinations, for there the life of the city is

Figure 5.14

Landmarks—the British
Parliament in London.
Landmarks are points of reference
that stand out in a landscape to
cue travel behavior. Big Ben, for
example, can be seen from many
parts of Westminster, enabling
sightseers to orient themselves as
they move through that section of
London.

focused at its most intensive pace. Sightseers see themselves as
potentially drawn.

"Landmarks" are points of reference. Activity is not actually
or even potentially focused on them. They serve primarily to
cue movement or to relate people to other elements in a landscape. They are clearly defined as figure against background
and, accordingly, their value lies in their clear visibility as an
attractor of the eye. They are especially useful to the conceptualization of city space when they are large and visible over
great distances.[31] Big Ben is an important landmark in
London, a city full of landmarks (fig. 5.14). Silhouetted beside
the Thames and visible from adjacent streets both motorists
and pedestrians easily cue their access to the Houses of
Parliament and adjacent Whitehall.

"Districts" are areas of a city that display a high degree of
homogeneity. They have some identifying character usually
reflected in physical structure and translated thereby into visual
image. Homogeneities of facade (especially material,
ornament, color, silhouette, and fenestration) may serve to
establish continuity in a sequence of views, thus establishing
a sense of regularity at a macroscale. Architecture of a like
tradition contains elements that carry over from building to
building, knitting them together into a single city fabric. In the
view over Boston's Charlestown, two districts are discernible:
the older traditional city of terrace houses facing the streets

with irregular backyards, and a newer public housing development focused away from the streets onto regular courtyards (fig. 5.15).

"Edges" are linear elements not used or considered as paths by the observer. They are boundaries, sometimes barriers, between two phases of landscape: for example, between two districts. Edges may perform an anchoring function to bind elements of a landscape together or they may serve a discriminating function to separate elements.[32] In the view over Chicago's "Gold Coast" the sense of edge pervades. Lake Michigan provides an obvious eastern limit to the city, but this sense of barrier is reinforced visually by the beach, Lake Shore Drive, and the line of high-rise apartment buildings that loom clifflike above the street (fig. 5.16).

Legibility is a function of movement. It results from things being seen over and over again so that they are raised to a high level of visual significance. Chicago's Michigan Avenue falls into place visually through the repetition of landscape components. Beginning in Grant Park the traditional Loop business district looms as a clear edge in the photograph (fig. 5.17). Once on the avenue a path opens up (fig. 5.18). Here the sightseer moves north, drawn by the city's new commercial node, the "miracle mile" signified by taller buildings in the distance. Individual structures, first viewed from a distance, affirm as landmarks the sightseer's course (fig. 5.19).

Landscapes are meant to be seen in movement. Built

Figure 5.16

Edges—Chicago, Illinois. The shore of Lake Michigan, Lake Shore Drive, and the wall of apartment facades facing the lake combine to provide a distinctive edge to the city. Edges are linear referents seen as bounding a landscape.

environments are not meant to be read or used as passive stage sets. The significative organization of a landscape is as temporal as it is spatial: settlements are designed to be construed spatially over time.[33] Paths, nodes, landmarks, districts, and edges provide the glue of serial vision. As constructs they serve to tie individual scenes together toward larger-scale definitions of scenery as place. As such they influence as carryover effect what is seen at any one moment. They are retained in memory as clearly legible aspects of landscape giving imageability to a city, small town, rural, or even wilderness, place.

BEAUTY IN COMPOSITION

Landscapes are not usually composed as works of art (designed parkland is an exception). As Ian Laurie writes, the criteria for assessing works of art, especially the artist's manifest skills and

Figures 5.17, 5.18, and 5.19
Legibility—Chicago, Illinois. A
city is necessarily comprehended
in movement: its most legible
elements seen in the repetition of
serial vision. Here facades of
Michigan Avenue form an edge
to the Loop, Chicago's traditional
business district and the city's
principal nodal area. The path of
Michigan Avenue leads the eye
from landmark to landmark.
Edge, district, node, path, and
landmark repeat in serial vision
making the city legible.

meanings, cannot be applied directly to most landscapes. Thus
the objects of landscape usually are not consciously grouped or
arranged, shaped, patterned, or colored for aesthetic effect.
However, sightseers or other observers can create their own
compositional effects. They can place themselves in positions
where landscapes appear to compose as art. Aesthetic appreciation of landscape varies with change in viewpoint and in the
opportunities available for viewing. What one sees at any
single moment not only reflects the reality of landscape as
material environment, but one's ability to internalize what is
seen as well. Laurie lists the factors that affect what one sees.

Some factors are innate (quality of vision, imagination, ability to contemplate); some are acquired (fashion and taste in society, education or training in landscape appreciation, and past place experience). Important also is the sightseer's receptivity (physical capabilities, general health, mood). The complexities of these factors create degrees of inconsistency in response both within and between individuals over time.[34]

Beauty sensed in a landscape, however, may well be a function of composition. George Santayana observes that the landscape cannot be enjoyed except through the mind actively relating its parts as "objectified emotion." "It has no real unity, and, therefore, requires to have some form or other supplied by the fancy; which can be the more readily done, in that the possible forms are many, and the constant changes in the object offer varying suggestions to the eye." "In fact, psychologically," he concludes, "there is no such thing as a landscape: what we call such an infinity of different scraps and glimpses given in succession." When the "scraps and glimpses" come together to compose in highly satisfying ways, then a sense of beauty may be thought to pervade.[35] Perhaps it is unwise to even discuss beauty in searching for the visual elements of landscape. Beauty is, after all, very much in the eye of the beholder. But I think that it is not unreasonable to claim that before a sense of beauty is derived, a landscape has to appear satisfying to the viewer. And that satisfaction is derived from a clear sense of prospect and refuge, an ease at handling visual details, and an ease at discovering the picturesque, i.e., defining scenery as pictures that readily compose to the eye.

Sightseers see landscape in the broad outlines of prospect and refuge. They search for the detail that gives place a sense of character. They also attempt to organize the whole as composition. Judgments accumulate through serial vision as certain general components of landscape repeat to sketch the outlines of encompassing geography. Much of this experience is not verbalized. Instead, sightseers engage in sight-thinking: an often unconscious sorting of views favoring those of pictorial value. A sense of the scenic, the sightseer's search for the picturesque, is rooted in the use of pictorial images, especially in reliance on photographic art. In the next chapter I explore how these pictures contribute to a sense of geography through the cognitive mapping of visual environment.

Chapter 6

Landscape
Visualization
and
Cognitive
Mapping

The foundations of
geographical knowledge lie in
the direct experience and
consciousness we have of the
world we live in.

EDWARD RELPH

The pictures that constantly impinge on consciousness form
a basis for geographical knowing. Mental pictures garnered
from landscape are synthesized as sightseers' personal
geography: the objects of landscape, as they form distinctive
place configurations, map into mental schema to orient sightseers by telling them where they are in an array of infinite
locational possibilities. Such cognitive mapping, as a thought
process, serves to identify at various geographical scales the
important places for the sightseeing at hand, to show how each
place relates spatially, and to suggest the satisfactions or dissatisfactions implicit. Cognitive mapping is essentially
problem solving. It keeps sightseers oriented to their surroundings so that movement becomes purposive. It serves to
predict place encounter so that the sightseers, as tourists, can
amplify place satisfaction. Thus sightseers link origins and
destinations, keep directions, and estimate distances. They
attach meaning to the environment categorized as behavioral
settings.

143

Behavioral geographers and environmental psychologists have suggested that cognitive mapping, including that of sightseeing, produces "mental maps" in an analogy to cartography. Sketch maps that people draw to orient themselves and others to an area have been analyzed as cognitive map surrogates. The schema of geographical location, they argue, is reflected in the sketch maps people draw and use.[1] This analogy to the map is unfortunate for it implies that people carry maps around in their heads. I suspect that whatever it is that people internalize in their minds, it is only rarely, if ever, a map. It is, rather, a process of thought that enables them to orient geographically. Occasionally, sketches or other kinds of maps, as devices handy for organizing and storing geographical information, are used to augment and perfect this thinking about places and their locations.

Cognitive mapping structures the information a sightseer holds about the geographical distribution of places so that movement between places is facilitated. It is a step-by-step associating of various place representations so that being in one place suggests how one might be in another. Stephen Kaplan writes: "Going from one representation to its associated 'next' representations may not seem very impressive, since it involves only a single predictive step. But from any next representation one can make still further predictions, since these representations have their associations in turn. This step–by–step pattern of associations thus defines a quite complex structure and permits predictive sequences that can be indefinitely long." The resulting "network of representations" constitutes a cognitive mapping of the environment.[2]

Students of cognitive mapping have generally ignored the visual aspects of environmental experience. They have not been interested in exploring how place identities are rooted in the seeing of landscape as visual display. David Canter justifies this neglect when he states that processes underlying dealings with places are essentially cognitive rather than perceptual. That is, cognitive mapping occurs after perception, or after the person's response to the stimulus of environment. He continues: "This has distinct implications for the [analysis] of maps because it suggests that it is the spatial arrangement of places not their visual organization which is crucial." Thus he would emphasize reality as map over reality otherwise revealed, as, for example, through pictures.[3] I choose a different approach. I see picture and map as integrally related. I believe that vividness of reality mentally pictured strongly influences the content of cognitive mapping. Perception and cognition cannot be separated if we are to comprehend fully how people conceptualize the world as geography. The sightseer's world serves to illustrate.

WAYFINDING

Sightseeing is a part of tourism whereby the traveler obtains visual stimulus. To some it may be a deliberate ritual performed as an act of travel. To others it may be merely a reflexive stance, a necessary part of touring. Travel is conducted at various scales of comprehension. Tourists first decide what kinds of places they want to visit in terms of broad categories of place meaning. They then choose specific destinations assessed either as attractions, logistical stops, or both. Planning is done in anticipation of travel, but most tourists also plan as they move, keeping options open in the search for pleasurable adventure. Tourist attractions are specially contrived places because they serve to heighten interest by focusing visitor attention through special interpretation. The pleasure trip is essentially the linking of tourist attractions in a circuit of outward and homeward movement.

Attractions are defined at various geographical scales. Whole landscapes (for example, large parks or, indeed, entire towns or regions) may be specially managed to attract visitors. Sightseeing, as landscape visualization, comes to the fore as the tourist moves between such attractions. Once a scenic or otherwise significant area has been reached, however, sightseeing also provides the means for assessing local ambience, for example, at the scale of the resort. A new set of attractions is prescribed in the locality and sightseeing renewed in locally directed movement. Resorts provide novel experiences variously packaged as attractions. The resort provides tourists with a matrix of potential involvements to be filled in with discoveries all their own.[4] It is sightseeing that provides much of the filler, with tourists validating their travel expectations primarily as onlookers. Through their search for scenic views sightseers validate and elaborate their cognitive mapping of touristic opportunity.

Tourists who arrive in a new town confront the place and the

Figure 6.1

Map orientation—Sauk Centre, Minnesota. Maps are indispensable to strangers orienting themselves to new places. This map orients sightseers to Sauk Centre by identifying key paths and edges. Sightseeing rarely starts without such a map. Maps direct seeing, visualization serving to validate expectations predicated on map use.

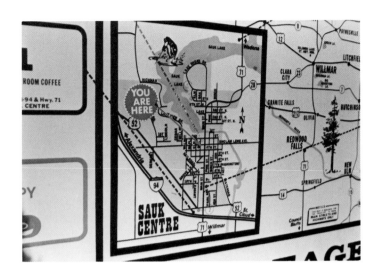

places that comprise it through wayfinding. They enter, by highway, railroad, or airport, and their first impressions form a framework for subsequent visualization. They come with directions because touring is rarely totally unplanned. Published maps are necessary for finding hotels and other logistical places; they are useful for finding museums, shops, parks, or other attractions (fig. 6.1). Certainly, the conventions of published cartography influence how people conceptualize an area as geography. Conventional maps exert influence over cognitive mapping just as photographs influence the sense of the picturesque. Tourists start with a general notion of how a landscape is spatially structured. They choose a path to begin exploration, to start their circuit of attractions. Using their eyes to pilot the way, the pictures mentally formed validate expected attractions as they are encountered, and identify new attractions discovered in passing.

Ideally, pictorial seeing validates the locational schema carried inside the sightseer's head. It offers elaboration resulting from direct observation of landscape. When the landscape does not provide the expected pictures the sightseer may become disoriented and even lost, and return to the published map or request new information from other sources. Revised cognitive mapping redirects serial vision as the information of each pictorial sequence once again validates movement as directed and purposeful. Wayfinding is the use of vision to establish rules for movement. It is a constant effort after spatial meaning.[5] It is a search for patterned relationships between places pictured in the mind as sorted geographically.

Wayfinding is the very essence of serial vision. The two are integrally linked in that one cannot exist without the other. James Gibson writes: "An alley in a maze, a room in a house, a street in a town, and a valley in a countryside each constitutes a place, and a place often constitutes a vista. . . . Vistas are serially connected since at the end of an alley the next alley opens up; at the edge of the doorway the next room opens up; at the corner of the street the next street opens up; at the brow of the hill the next valley opens up. To go from one place to another involves the opening up of the vista ahead and closing in of the vista behind." Wayfinding, therefore, involves the mental processing of emerging and occluding views. When vistas have been put in order by exploratory locomotion, Gibson continues, the invariant structure of the house, the town, or the whole habitat will be apprehended as a totality. "To the extent that one has moved from place to place, from vista to vista, one can stand still in one place and see where one is, which means where one is relative to where one might be."[6]

Wayfinding is comprised of the following steps: (1) orienting, (2) choosing the route, (3) keeping the right track, and (4) discovering the objective.[7] To orient is to relate oneself to some directional scheme (in/out, center/periphery, up/down, away/near), although to orient, in the strict sense of the word, means to face east, to face the rising sun. Getting one's bearings is to match one's orientation in a landscape to the appropriate maps, including one's cognitive schema. Visualization plays a vital role. Clues to direction are to be had in things seen: quality of light, length of shadow, positioning and density of buildings, width of streets, movement of people. Orienting enables directional choice, the first step in the sightseer's striking off across landscape in search of anticipated attractions (figs. 6.2 and 6.3).

In choosing the route one must first choose the mode of travel. One must decide to walk, ride a bus, drive a car, take a train. This decision hinges on the perceived distances involved, as suggested by a map or other authority, and the perceived time allotted, as dictated by one's priorities as tourist. With

Figures 6.2 and 6.3

Directional cues—Petersburg, Illinois, and Champaign, Illinois. For a visitor seeking the center of Petersburg, the cues are many: court house and business buildings in the middleground contrast with houses in the foreground. The slope downhill also points toward the center. In Champaign, as in most places, street signs uniformly declare cardinal directions.

mode of travel decided, tourists must tentatively choose that sequence of paths that will enable them to achieve their goals. They thus move along the anticipated routes, guiding themselves by the intermediary sights that indicate correct directions and distances traveled. Thus in keeping to the right track tourists constantly monitor their movements. Their changing views of landscape are directed toward those objects of place that reinforce the sense of forward progress. They search for the more legible aspects of place: the paths, nodes, landmarks, edges, and districts that suggest goal achievement. Thus a motorist moves along the path of Los Angeles' Wilshire

Figures 6.4 and 6.5
Keeping the right track—
Wilshire Boulevard, Los
Angeles, California. Landmarks
appear in sequence along paths
that reinforce a sense of steady
course. Here landmarks appear,
grow in size, and pass
peripherally as the motorist
proceeds.

Boulevard as pictured (figs. 6.4 and 6.5). Landmarks appear in the distance. Each looms in turn as approached and passes peripherally in a sequence of views directed along the street as vista. A sense of progress derives as landmarks validate expectations.

Views play an important role in goal discovery. Tourists may carry an image of an attraction in their minds based on photographs or other pictures seen. They may carry a verbal description or may operate solely on the basis of felt "place-type" derived from previous experiences elsewhere. An object seen will either fit or not fit the expectation. In either case, it

Figures 6.6 and 6.7

Seeking popularized views—
California's Yosemite National
Park. The road system of the park
gives access to all the principal
vantage points first made popular
by nineteenth-century
photographers. Tourists come
seeking these popularized views
as constituting the very essence of
Yosemite as a place. They do not
consider that they have seen
Yosemite until they experience
these views firsthand.

will be the seeing of the thing that will suggest success in piloting. Thus the ability to obtain attractions as goals in wayfinding is substantiated in visualization. Where images are based primarily on photographs, the attraction may not be recognized until viewed from the perspective of the photographer. Many scenic places are so stereotyped in photographic art that visitors feel successful as visitors only when one or two select views are obtained firsthand. Many tourist attractions are physically structured to readily provide visitors with widely popularized photographic views as, for example, in Yosemite National Park (figs. 6.6 and 6.7).

Through wayfinding the landscape is visually assessed. Tourists attain a selection of an area's attractions, both those anticipated and those discovered in passing. By piloting a landscape, with gaze set for key decision points in the path system, they are free to seek the picturesque: to absorb landscape composed as scenery. A landscape with clearly legible elements lends itself readily to cognitive mapping. Pictures compose and relate easily one to another in the serial vision of movement. Rules of relationship readily derive, and, as the various systems of relationship become more apparent with familiarity, sightseers are able to place increased attention on the detail of place. It is easier to savor landscape as pictorial composition by emphasizing in their viewing the sense of prospect and refuge naturally comforting to strangers in a new environment. Sightseers unconsciously develop a heuristic: a

general procedure for noting landscape as meaningful within the context of exploring it geographically.

Wayfinding may be likened to the scientist's posing of hypotheses. Theories about the location of places are built up inductively and tested deductively. This idea, first suggested by psychologist G. A. Kelly, holds that each and every experience, as it is "absorbed" by a person, is interpreted in the light of previous experience, expectancies, and anticipations until it "makes sense," a process he calls "construing." Thus cognitive maps, Amos Rapoport argues, can be seen as linked hypotheses, the testing of which in wayfinding involves fitting visual representations of place into an overall schema. As cognitive maps are built up over time, they become more complex and accurate. Once many places and ways of getting there are known they are ordered hierarchically, based on their significance and the frequency of interaction with them. Initially, a skeletal conceptualization is built relating places. This is modified by the continued testing of new bits of information against expectations. Ultimately, a relatively veridical, or at least operationally adequate, schema is achieved, which remains relatively stable.[8]

Touristic Role Playing

Sightseers' sense of geography through wayfinding reflects their backgrounds, their specific choices of attractions as goals, and, of course, their modes of travel. People bring to travel different personal histories: specific schooling, job experience, residential history. Obviously these differences influence what people see in a landscape and they influence even more the meanings attached to places visually identified. There are, however, certain behaviors that sightseers share as they play the role of tourist. These shared behaviors bring degrees of visual consensus to sightseeing which cut across social and cultural lines.

The tourist as stranger cannot know a locality as a resident might because the tourist's evaluation of place is essentially visual. He judges the look of things as they variously support or reject his place expectations. As a seeker after novelty, the tourist tends to focus on the unique qualities of place, especially scenic qualities, as they are pictured by him. There are, of course, different kinds of tourists. Sociologist Max Kaplan differentiates between two extremes: comparative strangers and emphatic natives.[9] Comparative strangers travel physically, but never, or seldom, change familiar viewpoints. They find security wherever they go by applying the popularly accepted standards of home to things seen. Emphatic natives seek by putting themselves in the place of those with whom they visit. They actively seek new viewpoints by seeing and then defining rather than by defining and then seeing. Most tourists fit somewhere between Kaplan's two poles but perhaps closer to the former than the latter. In both cases, however, it is seeing, no matter how insightful, that lays the basis for the experience of place. Seeing, not participating, is the essence of touristic experience. To actually participate as a native is to cease being a tourist.

Eric Cohen identifies five modes of touristic experience. The "recreational mode" is a quest for entertainment and within it tourists act as if attending a performance or participating in a game. Landscapes are seen not as part of the workaday world but as displays catering to visual excitement. Cohen's "diversionary mode" is escapist. Tourists travel, changing location, but continue to act very much as if at home. Places change only as visual arrays bringing superficial novelty. In the "experiential mode" tourists seek meaning from the lives of others by adopting elements of other life-styles. Such experiencing is largely by appearances only. In the "experimental mode" new life-styles are adopted for short periods. In the "existential mode" visitors cease being tourists by committing themselves to another way of life.[10] Recreational and diversionary modes dominate tourism and are largely visual or scenic in orientation. Again, seeing and not doing is of the essence in most touring.

Tourism is a use of leisure time. It is an antithesis of work filled with pleasant expectation and recollection. It represents a breaking of usual social ties and thus gives a sense of psychological freedom. Its orientations range from the inconsequential and insignificant to the weighty and important, although everything tends to be embraced through a sense of play. Tourists seek to escape from environments seen as mundane, to escape the drudgery of everyday places. They seek new experiences as an evaluation of self as they seek to enhance their status among acquaintances. They seek the sociability of those with whom they travel. Above all, tourists seek relaxation in pleasurable circumstances. Seeing, as a form of doing, is the essence of such experience. As onlooker the tourist uses new visual environments to achieve a sense of change. Visual environment, as it cues social meanings, puts him in distant and thus comfortable contact with the different kinds of people encountered. Different ways of life can be experienced with minimum psychic damage. The tourist does not have to commit; he only has to observe.[11]

Historian Daniel Boorstin sees tourism as blatantly stereotyped. "People," he writes, "go to see what they already know is there. The only thing to record, the only possible source of surprise, is their own reaction." To condemn the tourist for shallow experiences, however, is to miss the point of tourism. The tourist's role is essentially that of self-appraisal through seeing the world firsthand. He travels as an observer conceptualizing the world visually. Boorstin considers attractions to be "pseudo-events" or caricatures of reality. He sees touristic experiences as inauthentic when compared to the real experiencing of locals, the real occupants of place, who make profound social commitments to locality and thus know the real connotations. Thus attractions that pretend to show how the world works only reproduce reality as shadow. Contrived tourist attractions are merely displays offering intended messages, and reality thus becomes what the tourist is intended to see.[12] But what of the tourist's experiences between attractions? What of the insights of spontaneous sightseeing?

Sightseeing results in what Dean MacCannell calls "differentiations." Tourists differentiate society into its constituent parts based on unplanned encounters as they move through itineraries of travel. Identifying distinctive places as behavioral settings is one kind of differentiation. Indeed, an attraction as a touristic setting is merely one kind of place so distinguished. It is not the only kind of place encountered, but merely serves as a kind of goal encapsulating the tourist for extended periods of time. The seeing of sights between attractions, however, is not contrived. It is spontaneous. Unfortunately, little is known of the insights such sightseeing conveys. Until students of tourism carefully assess the significance of such seeing as knowing, judgment regarding tourism as superficial and unimportant might well be postponed.[13]

Attractions as Goals

Tourist attractions are places that most tourists readily recognize and accept as special. Place meaning is inherently touristic; that is, attractions are conceived and structured to be seen and otherwise experienced vicariously. Tourists are required only to look. Attractions exist to suit every taste although attractions of any given area tend to be similar or, at least, to complement one another as a resort complex. What tourists see of a given area, what they know of its landscape and the life it contains, is a function of the specific attractions they select. Such selection clearly reflects their backgrounds and the kind of tourists they intend to be. Nonetheless, the geographical scale of attractions potentially available in an area and their density also will influence a tourist's landscape awareness. The larger the scale the more noticeable and more widely experienced the attraction. The higher the density the more likely it is that an area's attractions will be selected as goals. The more attractions visited in an area, the more opportunity for spontaneous sightseeing between attractions. However, the larger the scale of an attraction, the greater the time spent there, meaning less time can be spent at other kinds of places.

Attractions packaged as highly stimulating visual displays may blind tourists to lesser scenery. The visual themes developed in an attraction may dominate seeing elsewhere. The outstanding vistas or panoramas of a place contrived for tourists may, like a photograph or other pictorial art form, stereotype vision; they lock the tourist into carrying these visions as models to sightseeing beyond. An attraction defined as goal, even when not yet seen, sets up expectations as to visual significance. Whereas tourist attractions may not represent the totality of touristic experience, it is clear that they exert considerable influence. They form the major points of attention around which cognitive mapping is formed. They dominate the basic cognitive schema with which sightseers anticipate landscape in their quest for scenery.

Mode of Travel

Mode of travel clearly influences what is seen of an area. The extent to which sightseers are exposed to the visual environment, the speed at which they move, and their ability to direct or control their movement all affect their visualization of landscape and their cognitive mapping of area. Pedestrians are open to the widest range of sensory stimulation whereas motorists are substantially buffered from the environment, encapsulated as they are within vehicles (figs. 6.8 and 6.9). An automobile's windows partially frame the landscape, thus directing vision. Pedestrians, on the other hand, move relatively slowly and can stop frequently to survey a given scene in detail. Feelings of being surrounded by the environment accrue to pedestrians who can turn to look in several directions. Motorists move rapidly and are restricted in their ability to stop and survey, and vision is directed forward. High-speed driving places severe restraints on the sightseer's ability to picture landscape because scenes present themselves too rapidly to be internalized, forcing the viewer to grossly simplify, for example, to focus on the broad outlines of scenery located at a distance. The passenger, whether in car, bus, or other form of transport, does not make route decisions. Reduced concern for piloting or navigating usually reduces the intensity with which landscape is visually surveyed, enhancing the ability to internalize scenery. However, scenes may be made less vivid because of the reduced need to orient and keep track.

Modes of travel that alienate the sightseer from landscape diminish cognitive mapping abilities. Travel by bus in a large city, as opposed to travel by underground train, may be expected to have a marked impact on the conception of the

Figures 6.8 and 6.9
Contrasting modes of travel—
trail in Utah's Bryce Canyon
National Park and highway near
Rolla in the Missouri Ozarks.
Pedestrians confront their
surroundings directly whereas
motorists are cocooned in metal
and glass quite apart from the
world outside.

city. The bus traveler has available a much wider range of cue
and information about the city, while the underground
traveler must rely more heavily on schematic representations.[14] The rider of surface transit reads the city in making his
way. The rider of the underground reads only a map. Riding
a subway in a city presents sightseers with dislocations that
severely disrupt their cognitive map. Exiting from an un-
familiar subway station to street level can be confusing as
tourists fight to reorient themselves to the landscape of the
street. They must reestablish a sense of direction and reset an
internal odometer in the calculation of distance.

PLACE UTILITY

Cognition results when sensory perceptions are sorted into
conceptual categories, including categories of place. Places are
identified by visual cue. The form of objects (both animate and
inanimate) and their relationships one to another enable
inferences to be made about the uses and consequences of a
given setting. Expected behavior, at least in general terms, is
predicted. For sightseers the most meaningful cues aid in wayfinding, validating expected attractions, and focusing attention
on the unexpected as intervening opportunities to pleasure.
People learn the likelihood of events occurring in their com-
merce with the environment and its redundant event

sequences. This predictive schema becomes their subjective model of the environment. Derived expectations focus their attention on objects that fit well their generalized representation. This particular state of perceptual readiness influences what they see and ultimately what they remember.[15]

Cognitive mapping grows through augmentation. It builds through successive layers of knowing. Expectations are posed and, if validated, strengthened. If invalidated, then new expectations rise to be tested. The cognitive map, according to Canter, involves four basic transformations by which the realities of landscape are internalized. First, the directions and distances of real space must be transformed into mental analogs. Even when viewed obliquely, objects of the visual environment must be known to retain constancy of form. Second, reality must be "miniaturized" in the mind so that objects may be grouped at the geographical scale of the city or the region. Third, a projection must be chosen whereby the normal eye-level viewpoint of daily experience can be converted into a "bird's-eye" map view. Finally, symbols must be used whereby objects in landscape consistently reflect in the mind as icons.[16] Augmentation in cognitive mapping proceeds along each line of transformation. Gibson would dispute Canter's third transformation. It is not so much having a bird's-eye view of the terrain as it is being everywhere at once. The getting of a bird's-eye view is helpful in becoming oriented, but orientation to goals behind walls, beyond the trees, and over the hill is not just a looking-down-on, and it is certainly not possession of a map assumed to exist in the mind. A map is a useful artifact when the hiker is lost, he asserts, but it is a mistake to confuse the artifact with the psychological state that the artifact promotes.[17]

Cognitive mapping functions as a predictive device. It not only serves to abstract and synthesize visual information, but, more important, it serves to predict behavior. People need to anticipate places as behavioral settings: to anticipate how their own behaviors are likely to fit. The sightseer, as tourist, needs to know where he is safe, where he is welcome, where he can be a sightseer. He needs to anticipate where sightseeing is likely to be most satisfying. The cognitive schema forming in his mind directs him in these discoveries. The locational schema provides the movement plan; it remains the basis for monitoring movement; it provides the basis for judging success in goal attainment. Therefore, cognitive mapping is biased toward the assessment of utility or function in landscape. The most important attribute of a place is its utility as a setting for behavior.

Sightseers as viewers of landscape search for prospect and refuge in the serial vision of wayfinding. Their eyes linger on details to compose and study pictures of the passing scene as they monitor their progress toward attractions known. The landscape as visualized is transformed into a cognitive schema of the area through which they move. Form in landscape provides the cues to finding the place utilities for which this schema is mentally constructed. Form is the essence of landscape visualized, but function, as the meaning attached, is the essence of geography cognized. Architect Raymond Curran writes: "It is not form itself that provides a source of meaning in our interpretation. Rather it is the function the form is seen to 'perform' and the clarity with which this is suggested that provides us meaningful information."[18]

Function readily follows form in carefully contrived landscapes. The cognitive mapping derived is simple and straightforward. Simple rules of association relate place form, as grouped objects, with place utility. Thus places are easily differentiated visually for the functions they perform. Physical forms act, when conceived within the context of clearly

Figure 6.10

Sign and place utility—Atlanta, Georgia. Cityscape and the signs orienting motorists to it often give conflicting messages. Here the motorist sees Atlanta's downtown to the left and yet the appropriate expressway exit is to the right. Here proper orientation is dependent upon signs.

established associations, as a language through which communication occurs. Contrived tourist attractions, for example, are structured to guide the visitor as onlooker through a sequence of obvious comprehensions. The place is easily conceptualized by the tourist because the satisfactions derived are overt and the tourist's role as actor readily anticipated. Expectations are easily validated toward pleasurable returns as function follows form by formula. However, beyond the comforting attractions of tourism the sightseer is left more on his own devices to find his way.

Confusion may reign where the semantic qualities of landscape are neglected and form and function not carefully associated. Landscape is irrelevant to the extent that people are uncertain of place meaning. An overreliance on signs results because a landscape that does not communicate through basic forms must communicate through sign.[19] Where movement is rapid and time to form clear pictures of place limited, signs are a necessity, as they are along the Atlanta freeway pictured in figure 6.10. Place utility is cued primarily by messages overtly verbalized rather than by messages of landscape subtly implied through form. Signs aid the sightseer as wayfinder, but may hinder the search for visual pleasure. Words may arrest the eye and the eye may fail to look beyond. The power of words displayed in a landscape can be strong, especially where forms are ambiguous.

Spaces architecturally designed are intended to readily

Figures 6.11 and 6.12
Contrasting place types—
Kalamazoo, Michigan, and
St. Andrews, New Brunswick.
Place utilities should be overtly
stated: a bank should look like a
bank, a church like a church.
Places, as behavioral settings,
should be cued visually in
consistent terms.

communicate visually place utility. Jan Mukarovsky notes five "horizons" of architecture by which function may be communicated. First, structure or form should communicate an immediate purpose. Viewers should recognize how a place is used and assess their own potential use of it. A bank should look like a bank, a church like a church (figs. 6.11 and 6.12). Second, form should imply a historical purpose wherein functionality is governed not only by an immediate practical consideration, but also by a fixed canon (or set of norms) regarding form of its type. For example, the traditional use of banks and churches as different kinds of places should be implicit. Third, manifestations of the social identity and territoriality of its makers and users should be evident. Fourth, the style within which the form is rendered should be obvious. Class and status may, in fact, be communicated by styling or sense of taste. Finally, Mukarovsky recognizes that not all

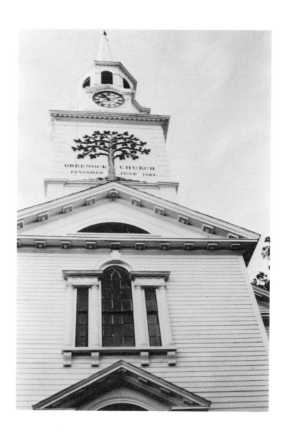

communicated meanings follow social convention. Individuals also assess architecture on purely personal, idiosyncratic bases. A person may become fond of specific landscape forms seemingly outside the public domain of sanctioned usage. Such feelings of topophilia, nonetheless, may be more widely shared within a society than its individuals are wont to admit.[20]

Buildings are remembered more for what they do than for how they look. Memory of a building, and thus the building's significance in cognitive mapping, appears to relate less to form or visual appearance than to utility or use, although visibility and ease of linguistic labeling are important also.[21] Buildings are expected to show how they can be used. People expect correspondence between visual properties and functional characteristics. Rudolf Arnheim writes: "Similar function should be reflected in similar shape; different functions in different shapes. Visual accents should occur in places of importance. The image of the building should lead, not

---

mislead, in its overall arrangement as well as detail."[22] What Arnheim describes could be applied by analogy to entire landscapes and to the qualities of landscapes that make for vivid cognitive mapping and a clear sense of geography.

PLACE CONSENSA

The sight-oriented roles associated with being a tourist, coupled with the inclination to see conventionally by analogy to pictures and maps, bring to sightseeing degrees of consensus. Place images, comprised of beliefs, attitudes, and icons, come to be widely shared.[23] Beliefs are understandings about places around which behavioral expectations are formed (the sense of place utility pervading) whereas attitudes are the associated positive or negative charges inclining people toward or away from places as behavior settings. Icons are features in landscape to which beliefs and attitudes attach. Icons are the objects of place cognitively pictured and mapped. They serve as clear symbols in the landscape of the beliefs and attitudes upon which place meaning is defined.

For sightseers, the sharing of place images, strong for some places and weak for others, reflects the manner by which tourist attractions are packaged and linked. It reflects the extent to which the sightseer's view is contained or directed through the contrivances of formulated attractions. Also, image sharing reflects the modes of travel available because in any given area sightseers tend to share a limited set of movement alternatives. Movement is limited to set approaches; attractions are linked in set ways. Sightseers bring beliefs and attitudes with them to the validation of places through direct seeing and the success of that validation determines the beliefs and attitudes taken away. The icons of place have associated with them degrees of satisfaction and dissatisfaction. To the extent that images are shared, there develops what Canter calls "consensa"; everybody's view or commonly held conceptualization of a place.[24]

Place consensa comprise clear mental "pictures" of place (especially pictures of the principal icons of place) and cognitive "maps" (especially schema built through wayfinding by which icons are linked spatially). Place consensa derive from symbolic interaction with the strongest consensa widely promoted through the media of popular culture. Published photographs and maps are, perhaps, the most important communicators about place in modern society. The images of places extensively publicized as tourist attractions may be so well known that travel becomes little more than an interacting with pictures and maps toward a firsthand validating or invalidating of expectations. Only with difficulty does one ignore intensive promotion of a place to form significant place conceptualizations distinctively one's own. However, in moving between attractions, the tourist's mind is more open to original discovery: the consensa of place being less developed, less widely shared, and less tyrannical accordingly.

What laypeople call geography is simply shared place consensa. It is information about places conceptualized analogously to pictures and to maps. The accuracy of such conceptualization, vis-à-vis the object world of reality, varies from person to person according to experience. Those with greater access to pictures and maps might be expected to hold a more comprehensive worldview. Those who travel most, whether as tourists or in playing other roles, might be expected to have greater geographical awareness. One's willingness to play the sightseer in travel (to consciously amplify concern for scenery) would be expected to have profound effect on geographical competency. Professional geographers aside, most people are probably biased toward the pictorial knowing of a place rather than the cognitive mapping of it. It is landscape as visualized that likely most influences place comprehension. I shall hypothesize that for most laypeople location is less significant than the other characteristics of place. This does not mean that people do not have a sense of geography. It means only that landscape is translated into a sense of geography through sight-thinking where the icons of place, as pictured, dominate their conceptual linkages as map.

Through wayfinding people link significant places in mapping cognitively the environment. Sightseers, as tourists, link attractions in their pilgrimages of pleasure. What they see reflects the role they play and the way they move. Places have utility for the visual pleasure they convey. The significant icons of place are linked positively to notions of adventure and relaxation. Through travel, especially in the more spontaneous interactions with landscape between contrived attractions, sightseers build a stock of impressions to fill out their geography of the world. Through visualization, landscape serves as a basis for geographical knowing. This relationship, although recognized by cultural geographers and other students of landscape, has not been adequately explored. In the concluding chapter, I suggest some directions which that exploration might take.

Chapter 7

Conclusion

The world is but canvas to
our imagination.

HENRY DAVID THOREAU

Published writings that deal with the visual landscape tend to
be speculative. They represent highly personal views of
authors who have sought to comprehend what they see in
landscape. So also this book has been conceived and written as
a personal search for lexicon. Built upon my own abilities at
visualizing landscape, I have sought to comprehend the act
I call sightseeing. I have canvassed a varied literature in search
of basic concepts: what I call the visual elements of landscape.
I have explored the observations of a wide range of authors
who have talked about the visual environment in vocabulary
that is meaningful to how I see the world. I have sought to
illustrate these concepts in photographs. In concluding, I offer
some speculations on how research and design might be
focused on the sightseeing impulse, and on the related visual
elements of landscape identified.

My exploration has demonstrated, I believe, that different
disciplinary points of view are not mutually exclusive. There

165

is, in fact, a single continuum. What architects perceive regarding a person's visualization of buildings, for example, can be applied to a geographer's comprehension of people's cognitive mapping of areas, and vice versa. The insights of environmental psychologists, art historians, photographers, landscape architects, and the host of other students of visual environment may yet be brought together in a field theory of landscape visualization. Clearly, no theory of landscape visualization yet exists. As Barry Sadler and Allen Carlson note, "no organized body of theory or even common definitions are yet available." With the present theoretical vacuum, Jay Appleton observes, the student of landscape visualization, in effect, starts from the same place as the person in the street. Beyond the general recognition that certain landscapes are more visually attractive than others no consensus exists on the relevant foci of aesthetic significance in the environment and the different acts of interpretation they demand.[1]

Although landscape visualization is a topic that potentially embraces all kinds of human activity, I would focus attention on sightseeing. It is sightseers who actively and deliberately engage their environment on visual terms. Relaxation, pleasure, edification are what is sought in places deliberately encountered for their visual novelty. The instinctual tendency to accept surroundings as functionally given has, with the sightseer, a decidedly visual basis. It is by providing an opportunity for the pleasurable seeing of things that places achieve their greatest value. Sightseers, as questors of visual aesthetics, are inclined to rise above mere acceptance and demand pleasurable stimulation. Justification for enhanced visual aesthetics through design derives overtly from the sightseers' quests. It is on sightseers, therefore, that future theory building initially might focus.

Sightseeing should be viewed as a form of role playing. What are the specific behaviors associated with this activity and how do they influence what is seen? Are there different styles or forms of sightseeing? How are these styles learned? How is sightseeing related to other kinds of activities? How is it related to personality? Are some people more inclined to the visual appreciation of environment than others? Are there cyclical or other temporal dimensions to sightseeing that influence what is seen? In what kinds of landscape does sightseeing flourish? Are there archetypal landscapes significant to sightseeing? Just how do sightseers define place significance? Finally, how does sightseeing vary from culture to culture, society to society? What are the universals? What are the important differences from group to group?

What I have suggested as universal in landscape visualization may be posed as a series of theorems for testing. The first theorem is: *People seek prospect and refuge as a basic framework for landscape visualization.*

Is the quest for prospect and refuge real or is Appleton's conceptualization more poetic than actual?[2] It is clear that the search for views constitutes the essence of sightseeing. The landscape first is established as a visual display through the serial linking of views. The extent of a view, or the distance seen, the sense of multiple horizons as anchored by focal points, and the sense of enframement all contrive to make some scenes more vivid than others. But how does this work for the average individual? What is it that makes one scene more memorable? How do the different kinds of vistas play out individually and in sequence to make one place more imageable than another? How does the urban street or rural road function to channel vision under various circumstances? How does motion affect the defining of vantage points and secondary vistas? It is less clear how the quest for refuge relates to sightseeing. What makes for effective enclosure? Can sightseers really sense fields of force operating in enclosed spaces? How significant is the sense of rest and safety communicated by enclaves and points of pause?

A second theorem is: *A landscape is seen to have character through discovery of its details.*

Is the quest for sense of place real or are the concerns of such authors as Lawrence Durrell, Christian Norberg-Schultz, and Yi-Fu Tuan overstated?[3] How do sightseers define scale in landscape? Are there, indeed, sets of expectations whereby the details of landscape are deemed appropriate? Do sightseers define romanticism in landscape in such terms as *spontaneity, complexity, contraposition, surprise,* and *mystery?* Is classicism seen to play out as *order, simplicity, balance, harmony?* How does the sightseer react to rhyme and rhythm? Is there such a thing as "face" in landscape? How do changing light and color affect what is seen and remembered of a place?

A third theorem is: *Landscapes are viewed as pictorial compositions.*

What are the compositional "fixes" that sightseers use in seeking scenery? To what extent do the conventions of landscape painting and landscape photography exert an influence on what is seen in everyday places? How does the recognition of unity, enframement, balance, focal center, or the sense of entrance/exit excite a sense of scenic value? Is there such a thing as sight-thinking and can it be measured in compositional terms? Are such authors as Kevin Lynch correct in their defining of legibility in landscape?[4] Are landscapes viewed and remembered primarily in terms of paths, nodes, landmarks, districts, and edges? Or are there other devices, yet unrecognized, that better serve the needs of pictorial composition in serial vision?

A fourth theorem is: *Visual images of landscape contribute to geographical awareness through cognitive mapping.*

How do the processes of wayfinding (choosing the route, keeping the right track, and discovering the objective) affect what is seen? What kinds of places serve as primary attractors? How do attractions defined at different scales relate as cognized geography? How do the cognitive mapping abilities of sightseers affect what is seen? How is place utility defined? And what kinds of place consensa emerge among sightseers as a class of place user in given locales? How do the visual images of landscape contribute to geographical knowing?

Academics in North America have put little value on sightseeing as a social role and they have discounted tourism as a kind of social activity. Both the United States and Canada were wrought from wilderness conditions producing not only a strong work ethic but also a strong utilitarian orientation to landscape, rooted in what geographer David Lowenthal calls the "pioneer impulse."[5] How things look matters little. How things work or will work in the future matters more. The place impressions of tourists are assumed by scholars to be superficial in contrast to those of natives, the assumed doers and movers of society.[6] Touristic orientations to landscape have been viewed as essentially aesthetic, a mere seeing of place as opposed to full experiencing. Landscape aesthetics have been more highly valued in Europe as a scholarly pursuit. European elites have been adroit at creating visually aesthetic landscapes expressive of social control. The look of places and the functioning of places are more equally valued, the one seen to

---

reflect upon the other.[7] Tourism is prized as an activity, but even more as an industry, and the latter is in large measure sustained by aesthetically deprived Americans traveling abroad in search of visual pleasure.

Scholars, irrespective of how they value tourism, will benefit by focusing on sightseeing as a form of environmental experience. Every academic discipline rests on what I call an experiential base. It is a foundation of observation rooted in the values of society. It comprises the principal ways of knowing, assessing, evaluating, identifying, acknowledging, discovering, noticing. It is a part of the popular culture of a people, rooted in their linguistics, their history, their ideologies. Various academic disciplines extract from this base of experience conceptual and theoretical frameworks for enhanced understanding or comprehension; the first concepts and the first theories extracted impose a tyranny of precedence on subsequent disciplinary evolution. Theory serves scientists to predict the behavior of phenomena in the universe, including that of humans. Theory serves the artist, on the other hand, in effectuating emotional and other responses in human audiences. The scientist is order seeking, the artist order imposing. Above the experiential base and conceptual/theoretical levels stands an experimental/analytical level where hypotheses are tested. Patterns and relationships are assessed: scientists seek cause and effect whereas artists seek effectual expression. At the top of every pyramid of knowledge there is an ultimate level of practical application. Here tested generalizations are translated into social policy and/or physical environmental design. Each of the higher levels feeds back into the experiential base to influence what passes as common knowledge. Indeed, a discipline's applied phase is fully intended to have such impact. Only with great difficulty, however, do scholars return to the experiential base in search of new points of view. Society's view of the world may change, societal needs may be redefined, but many academic disciplines, especially those with weak feedback loops, may continue, despite these changes, to formulate and reformulate old questions. As historians of science such as Thomas Kuhn have established, true shifts of paradigm are come by with great difficulty.[8]

Academic concern with the sightseer is first and foremost

a concern with the scholar's disciplinary base. For academic geography, which is traditionally focused on the form and function of landscape as object reality, the focus on sightseeing may require a shift of paradigm. It is not object reality that is important. Rather, it is the impression of that reality as conveyed through the process of seeing that is at issue. The geographer, as student of landscape, must necessarily refocus on images of place, especially visual images that cue place meaning. Accordingly, new questions regarding the visualization of landscape need to be asked. Of course, emphasis on sightseeing can be a challenge to other disciplines as well. Architects might refocus on the public's experiencing of buildings in landscapes instead of continuing their traditional preoccupation with structures as design isolates. They might analyze the behavior of users, relating that behavior to total design. Psychologists, for their part, might emphasize human behavior as observed in actual landscapes rather than focusing on behavior contrived in laboratories. The sightseer's spontaneous assessment of landscape, as a research focus, invites innovation in various disciplinary contexts.

The design implications of research focused on the visual elements of landscape are substantial. Certainly an understanding of sightseeing as a process of landscape visualization has much to contribute to the design of resorts. Understandings, however, hold implications beyond the design of touristic places. By knowing what people find visually satisfying in landscapes, visually pleasing environments can be created to contain a wide variety of human activities. Much of the expertise brought to bear on new towns and planned unit developments in Europe and North America has been based on design intuition rooted in traditional design vocabularies rather than in the real knowing of what people actually see as attractive. Designed landscapes are conceived in the abstract on paper or in models to appeal to the designer's eye. A concern with sightseer experiences represents, it seems to me, a prime mechanism for enriching design inspiration.[9] Research on landscape visualization also can be brought to bear on the modification of existing landscapes. It can suggest what is visually significant and thus ought to be saved or enhanced. It can identify weak visual relationships in landscapes and suggest where new construction ought to be or ought not to be inserted.

Americans tend to be indifferent to good design in the visual environment. Writing in the 1890s, George Santayana observed that "it does not occur to them that the work-a-day world is capable of aesthetic contemplation. Only on holidays, when they add to themselves and their belongings some unusual ornament, do they stop to watch the effect." Lynch observed in the 1960s that not one urban place in the United States larger than a village is "of constantly.fine quality." He writes: "[Americans] are hardly aware of the potential value of harmonious surroundings, a world which they have briefly glimpsed only as tourists or as escaped vacationers." As Lynch maintains, Americans have little sense of what landscape can mean in terms of daily delight, or as a continuous anchor for their lives. The American experience with sightseeing, however, does provide a context where better environmental design, experientially based, might begin.[10]

What constitutes an attractive visual landscape? This is the question that designers need to ask and answer. What comprises visual interest? Visual excitement? Visual satisfaction? How does the visual environment break down into constituent parts and how do these parts combine in satisfying ways? Scholars across various academic disciplines can contribute to the understanding of such landscape aesthetics. Only a few basic premises seem necessary. First, scholars need to recognize that seeing is important to human well-being. Such activities as sightseeing can be of substantial social significance. Second, landscapes need to be studied as visual displays with form and function held as related but subsidiary concerns. Third, research needs to focus on individuals as they experience landscape in order to learn how it is that people actually do confront environment as visual display. Scholars and designers need to think of landscape as a process of visualization.

This book has grown out of my own experience as sightseer. Comprehending landscape as visual display was not something that came easily. It was a new role requiring a distinctly new scholarly orientation. As a geographer I was educated to see specific things in landscape that varied geographically, cueing functional meaning. I focused on those features in landscape clearly rooted in the past that reflected cultural history. As Donald Meinig says in his article "Environmental Appreciation: Localities as a Humane Art," the cultural geographer regards landscapes as "intricate continuous surfaces which display changing styles and tastes, technologies and functions; which are in turn expressions of our cultural values, our really basic ideologies."[11] With this orientation I sought to record observations with photographs in order to build a visual archive of landscape appreciation. A camera became an adjunct to my seeing, and, ultimately, an instrument of changing viewpoint.

For years my photographs showed things in the landscape such as houses, barns, skyscrapers. These photographs were taken because particular structures were somehow significant in function or reflected cultural change. I then began to reorient my emphasis. As a geographer, wasn't I supposed to study spatial relationships? Shouldn't I be photographing the spatial proximity of things in landscape? Shouldn't I be seeing and photographing things as they fit into larger spatial contexts? A first step in redirecting my vision was to photograph spaces, to deliberately seek out and picture the openness of roads, plazas, and areas across which specific structures related. Space, I discovered, was defined visually according to the way solids (or the things of substance that had previously dominated my thinking) provided visual boundedness. To effectively picture a space, I learned, one had to lead the eye toward, into, across, and out of the void using peripheral objects as visual cues. This was the beginning of my interest in the visual elements of landscape.

Spaces are filled with people, their activities, and their activity props, and I realized that I was not photographing "space" so much as "place." I discovered that in many instances the cues to pictorial success obtained through the camera's viewfinder were the same cues to place identity that made places seem attractive to me. I began seeing aesthetic relationships in landscape that I had never seen before. I began photographing scenes purely for visual satisfaction totally divorced from any sense of discovered cultural landscape significance. I began seeking out places that appeared aesthetically pleasing. I next began to study scenes that I found lacking in visual satisfaction. Out of this experimentation came identification of many of the elements of visual landscape cited above.

I would ask that every student of landscape explore the

sightseer within. Ask yourself what constitutes an aesthetically pleasing landscape. What do you see as attractive in a place? What kinds of scenes attract most? Think also about what you find unattractive, and about the kinds of places that neither attract nor repulse, but pass totally unseen or unremembered. Your thinking should embrace places defined at different scales, and places used for different purposes. It should embrace both planned and unplanned landscapes. How significant to your seeing are the various elements of visual landscape? How effectively, for example, is a place announced visually? How effectively does the visual composition lead you into, through, and out of a place? What strikes the eye as most effective in defining prospect? What kinds of vistas predominate? Where does the eye focus and how are vantage points cued? To what extent does a sense of refuge pervade? What are the significant details that give character to place? What readily composes as picturesque? How readily are things anticipated in the cognitive mapping of landscape?

This reading and interpreting of landscape is not a search for higher levels of form and function, a search for landscapes as macro objects. It is not an attempt to reclassify structures and their associated utilities into progressively higher orders of settlement notation. It is instead an attempt to identify how things relate visually and, on the basis of these visual relationships, to identify significant patterns of aesthetic meaning. It means going back to investigate how one sees landscape defined as visual display. It means thinking about the rudiments of how one sees places. It means a rethinking of visual experience whereby landscapes are encountered firsthand. I call for a kind of counterinduction whereby the apparent visible facts of landscape are ignored in the search for new landscape comprehensions.

Notes

PREFACE

1   John B. Jackson, *Discovering the Vernacular Landscape* (New Haven: Yale University Press, 1984), p. x.

2   Richard Hartshorn, *The Nature of Geography* (Lancaster, Penn.: Association of American Geographers, 1939), p. 152. Denis E. Cosgrove, *Social Formation and Symbolic Landscape* (London: Croom Helm, 1984), p. 16.

3   David Lowenthal, "Finding Valued Landscapes," *Progress in Human Geography* (1978):373–410; see esp. p. 375.

I   INTRODUCTION

1   E. Relph, *Place and Placelessness* (London: Pion, 1976), p. 56.

2   Yi-Fu Tuan, *Space and Place: The Perspective of Experience* (Minneapolis: University of Minnesota Press, 1977), p. 6.

3   Relph, *Place and Placelessness*, p. 29.

4   My notion of place rests on the "behavior setting" formulation of psychologist Roger Barker. To Barker, behavior settings, as centers of behavioral intention, consist of "standing patterns of

behavior-and-milieu." See Roger G. Barker, *Ecological Psychology* (Stanford: Stanford University Press, 1968), p. 18.

5   John Donat, ed., *World Architecture 4* (London: Studio Vista, 1967), p. 9.

6   Tuan, *Space and Place,* p. 161; Christian Norberg-Schultz, *Genius Loci: Towards a Phenomenology of Architecture* (New York: Rizzoli, 1980), p. 6.

7   Amos Rapoport, *Human Aspects of Urban Form* (Oxford: Pergamon Press, 1977), p. 326. See also Peter F. Smith, *The Syntax of Cities* (London: Hutchinson, 1977), p. 17.

8   Yi-Fu Tuan, *Topophilia: A Study of Environmental Perception, Attitudes, and Values* (Englewood Cliffs, N.J.: Prentice-Hall, 1974), p. 63.

9   Dean MacCannell, *The Tourist: A New Theory of the Leisure Class* (New York: Schocken, 1976), p. 1.

10   Niels Prak, *The Visual Perception of the Built Environment* (Delft, Netherlands: Delft University Press, 1977), p. 71.

11   Rudolf Arnheim, *Visual Thinking* (Berkeley: University of California Press, 1969), pp. 229, 238.

12   Grady Clay, *Close-up: How to Read the American City* (New York: Praeger, 1973), pp. 19, 22; Kenneth Clark, *Looking at Pictures* (New York: Holt, Rinehart, and Winston, 1960), p. 16; Tuan, *Space and Place,* p. 6.

13   Arnheim, *Visual Thinking,* p. 246.

14   M. Krampen, *Meaning in the Urban Environment* (London: Pion, 1979), p. 34. Such an interpretation follows from the classic definition of semiotics. See C. Morris, *Signs, Language and Behavior* (New York: Braziller, 1955).

15   Donald Preziosi, *Architecture, Language and Meaning* (The Hague: Mouton, 1979), p. 3.

16   Ibid.

2   VISUALIZING LANDSCAPE

1   Yi-Fu Tuan, *Topophilia: A Study of Environmental Perception, Attitudes and Values* (Englewood Cliffs, N.J.: Prentice-Hall, 1974), p. 11; Jay Appleton, *The Experience of Landscape* (London: Wiley, 1975), p. 53.

2   Rudolf Arnheim, *Visual Thinking* (Berkeley: University of California Press, 1969), pp. 136, 148.

3   E. De Bono, *The Mechanism of Mind* (London: Cape, 1969), p. 41.

4   Amos Rapoport, *The Meaning of the Built Environment: A Nonverbal Communication Approach* (Beverly Hills, Calif.: Sage, 1982), pp. 14, 57, 62.

5   Peter F. Smith, *The Dynamics of Urbanism* (London: Hutchinson, 1974), p. 17.

6   De Bono, *Mechanism of Mind,* pp. 31, 40.

7   Ibid., pp. 181, 213.

8   Peter F. Smith, *The Syntax of Cities* (London: Hutchinson, 1977), p. 36.

9   For syntheses of the sensory perception literature relevant to visualization see James L. Gibson, *The Perception of the Visual World* (Boston: Houghton Mifflin, 1950); William H. Ittelson, *Visual Space Perception* (New York: Springer, 1960); William H. Segall, Donald T. Campbell, Melville J. Herskovits, *The Influence of Culture on Visual Perception* (Indianapolis: Bobbs-Merrill, 1966); R. H. Day, *Human Perception* (Sydney: Wiley, 1969); Lloyd Kaufman, *Perception: The World Transformed* (New York: Oxford University Press, 1979).

10   Day, *Human Perception*, p. 2.

11   Ibid., p. 44.

12   Kevin Lynch, *The Image of the City* (Cambridge: M.I.T. Press, 1960), p. 106.

13   Amos Rapoport and Ron Hawkes, "The Perception of Urban Complexity," *American Institute of Planners Journal* 36 (1970): 109.

14   Jean Piaget and Barbel Inhelder, *The Child's Conception of Space*, trans. F. J. Langdon and J. L. Lunzer (New York: Norton, 1967), pp. 155–60.

15   Robert Beck, "Spatial Meaning and the Properties of the Environment," in *Environmental Perception and Behavior*, ed. David Lowenthal (Chicago: University of Chicago, Department of Geography, Research Paper no. 109, 1967), p. 18.

16   Piaget and Inhelder, *Child's Conception of Space*, p. 3.

17   Ibid.

18   For a similar typology focused on children's architectural involvements in place making, see Jose M. Thornberg, "Towards an Epistemology of Architectural Design as a Place-Making Activity," in *Meaning and Behavior in the Built Environment*, ed. Geoffrey Broadbent, Richard Bunt, and Tomas Llorens (Chichester, U.K.: Wiley, 1980), p. 186.

19   Yi-Fu Tuan, *Space and Place: The Perspective of Experience* (Minneapolis: University of Minnesota Press, 1977), p. 29.

20   Ibid.

21   Ibid.

22   For a description of children's place-specific behavior, see Roger Hart, *Children's Experience of Place* (New York: Irvington, 1978).

23   D. W. Meinig, ed., *The Interpretation of Ordinary Landscapes* (New York: Oxford University Press, 1979), p. 3; E. Relph, *Place and Placelessness* (London: Pion, 1976), p. 8.

24   Tuan, *Space and Place*, pp. 6, 12, 54.

25   Christian Norberg-Schultz, *Genius Loci: Towards a Phenomenology of Architecture* (New York: Rizzoli, 1980), pp. 11, 16, 19.

26   Tuan, *Space and Place*, p. 18.

27   Robert J. Yudell cited in Kent C. Bloomer and Charles W. Moore, *Body, Memory, and Architecture* (New Haven: Yale University Press, 1977), p. 57.

28   Ian Nairn, *The American Landscape: A Critical View* (New York: Random House, 1965), p. 5.

29   See Rapoport, *Meaning of the Built Environment*, p. 197.

30   Nairn, *American Landscape*, p. 45.

31   Relph, *Place and Placelessness*, p. 35.

32   Appleton, *Experience of Landscape*, p. 5; Tuan, *Topophilia*, p. 64.

33   Relph, *Place and Placelessness*, pp. 53–55.

34   John Ewart, "Art Environment and Education," in *The Aesthetics of Landscape*, ed. Jay Appleton (Didcot, U.K.: Rural Planning Services, 1980), p. 90.

35   Appleton, *Experience of Landscape*, p. 169. Carl G. Jung, *Seelenproblem Der Gegenwart* (Zurich: Rascher, 1931), p. 173, quoted in Smith, *Dynamics of Urbanism*, p. 56.

36   Stephen Kaplan, "Attention and Fascination: The Search for Cognitive Clarity," in *Humanscape: Environment for People*, ed. Stephen Kaplan and Rachel Kaplan (North Scituate, Mass.: Duxbury, 1978), p. 85.

3   LANDSCAPE AS PROSPECT AND REFUGE

1   Various authors have emphasized views in attempting to categorize landscapes as visual displays. R. Burton Litton, Jr. (*Forest Landscape Description and Inventories* [n.p.: USDA Forest Service Research Paper, PSW–49, 1968], p. 2) emphasizes six analytical factors: (1) distance; (2) observer position; (3) form; (4) spatial definition; (5) light; (6) sequence. Tadahiko Higuchi (*The Visual and Spatial Structure of Landscapes* [Cambridge: M.I.T. Press, 1983], p. 4) identifies seven factors: (1) visibility/invisibility (what can or cannot be seen); (2) distance; (3) angle of incidence (the angle at which the line of vision strikes a surface viewed); (4) depth of invisibility (the depth of the unseen over which the eye skips); (5) angle of depression/elevation (the viewer's sense of position as he looks down or up toward an object); (6) depth (the sense of three-dimensionality); and (7) light. In chapter 3 I deal only with those factors that influence the sense of prospect and refuge.

2   Paul D. Spreiregen, *Urban Design: The Architecture of Towns and Cities* (New York: McGraw-Hill, 1965), p. 71.

3   Gyorgy Kepes, *Language of Vision* (Chicago: Theobald, 1969), p. 87.

4   James J. Gibson, *The Ecological Approach to Visual Perception* (Boston: Houghton Mifflin, 1979), p. 147; Higuchi, *Visual and Spatial Structure of Landscape*, p. 62.

5   Jay Appleton, *The Experience of Landscape* (London: Wiley, 1975), p. 169.

6   Gordon Cullen, *The Concise Townscape* (New York: Van Nostrand Reinhold, 1976), p. 43. See also James F. Barker, Michael W. Fazin, and Hank Hildebrandt, *The Small Town as Art Object* ([Starkville, Miss.], 1975), p. 84.

7   Cullen, *Concise Townscape*, p. 43; Ian Nairn, *The American Landscape: A Critical View* (New York: Random House, 1965), p. 128; Barker, Fazin, and Hildebrandt, *Small Town as Art Object*, p. 44; Appleton, *Experience of Landscape*, p. 91.

8   Cullen, *Concise Townscape*, p. 46; Barker, Fazin, and Hildebrandt, *Small Town as Art Object*, p. 28.

9   Cullen, *Concise Townscape*, p. 41; Donald Appleyard, Kevin Lynch, and John R. Meyer, *The View from the Road* (Cambridge: M.I.T. Press, 1963), p. 14.

10   Cullen, *Concise Townscape*, p. 37; Barker, Fazin, and Hildebrandt, *Small Town as Art Object*, p. 74.

11   Appleton, *Experience of Landscape*, p. 88.

12   Ibid., p. 89.

13   Ibid., p. 199.

14   Rudolf Arnheim, *The Dynamics of Architectural Form* (Berkeley: University of California Press, 1977), p. 76; Amos Rapoport, *Human Aspects of Urban Form* (Oxford: Pergamon Press, 1977), p. 81.

15   Barrie B. Greenbie, *Spaces: Dimensions of the Human Landscape* (New Haven: Yale University Press, 1981), p. 41; Yoshinobu Ashihara, *The Aesthetic Townscape*, trans. Lynne E. Riggs (Cambridge: M.I.T. Press, 1983), p. 46; Arnheim, *Dynamics of Architectural Form*, p. 125; Rapoport, *Human Aspects of Urban Form*, p. 182.

16   Appleton, *Experience of Landscape*, p. 91; Barker, Fazin, and Hildebrandt, *Small Town as Art Object*, p. 70.

17   Peter F. Smith, *The Dynamics of Urbanism* (London: Hutchinson, 1974), p. 191.

18   Higuchi, *Visual and Spatial Structure of Landscapes*, p. 36. Higuchi's comments are based on Henry Dreyfuss (*The Measure of Man: Human Factors in Design* [New York: Whitney Publication, 1959]).

19   Arnheim, *Dynamics of Architectural Form*, p. 33; Barker, Fazin, and Hildebrandt, *Small Town as Art Object*, p. 74; Appleton, *Experience of Landscape*, p. 95; Cullen, *Concise Townscape*, pp. 39, 107; Peter F. Smith, *The Syntax of Cities* (London: Hutchinson, 1977), p. 89.

20   Grady Clay, *Close-up: How to Read the American City* (New York: Praeger, 1973), p. 53; Smith, *Syntax*, p. 129.

21   Appleton, *Experience of Landscape*, pp. 94, 105.

22   Smith, *Dynamics*, p. 141.

23   Appleton, *Experience of Landscape*, p. 121.

24   Ibid., p. 121; Jay Appleton, "Pleasure and the Perception of Habitat: A Conceptual Framework," in *Environmental Aesthetics: Essays in Interpretation,* ed. Barry Sadler and Allen Carlson (Victoria: University of Victoria, Department of Geography, Western Geographical Series, vol. 20, 1982), p. 39.

25   Cullen, *Concise Townscape*, pp. 33, 47; Raymond J. Curran, *Architecture and the Urban Experience* (New York: Van Nostrand Reinhold, 1983), pp. 69, 109.

26   Curran, *Architecture and the Urban Experience*, p. 112.

27   Ashihara, *Aesthetic Townscape,* p. 57.

28   Arnheim, *Dynamics of Architectural Form,* p. 85.

29   Ibid., pp. 16, 26.

30   Greenbie, *Spaces,* p. 41; Arnheim, *Dynamics of Architectural Form,* p. 33.

31   Spreiregen, *Urban Design,* p. 75.

32   Cullen, *Concise Townscape,* p. 25.

33   Robert Venturi, *Complexity and Contradiction in Architecture* (New York: Museum of Modern Art, 1967), p. 88; Arnheim, *Dynamics of Architectural Form,* p. 94.

34   Ashihara, *Aesthetic Townscape,* p. 49; Yi-Fu Tuan, *Topophilia: A Study of Environmental Perception, Attitudes, and Values* (Englewood Cliffs, N.J.: Prentice-Hall, 1974), p. 27.

35   Rapoport, *Human Aspects of Urban Form,* p. 246.

36   Arnheim, *Dynamics of Architectural Form,* p. 156.

37   Gibson, *Ecological Approach to Visual Perception,* pp. 197, 221.

38   Lawrence Halprin, *Cities* (Cambridge: M.I.T. Press, 1972), p. 197.

39   Appleyard, Lynch, and Meyer, *View from the Road,* p. 4.

40   Ibid., pp. 6–8.

41   Ibid., p. 14.

42   Rapoport, *Human Aspects of Urban Form,* p. 243.

43   Barker, Fazin, and Hildebrandt, *Small Town as Art Object,* p. 30.

4   CHARACTER IN LANDSCAPE

1   Lawrence Durrell, *Spirit of Place: Letters and Essays on Travel,* ed. Allan G. Thomas (New York: Dutton, 1969), pp. 158–60.

2   Yi-Fu Tuan, *Topophilia: A Study of Environmental Perception, Attitudes, and Values* (Englewood Cliffs, N.J.: Prentice-Hall, 1974), p. 4; Ian Nairn, *The American Landscape: A Critical View* (New York: Random House, 1965), p. 63; Christian Norberg-Schultz, *Genius Loci: Towards a Phenomenology of Architecture* (New York: Rizzoli, 1980), p. 18.

3   Henry S. Canby, "Traveling Intelligently in America," in *Essays of Today (1926–1927),* ed. Odell Shepard and Robert Hillyer (New York: Century, 1928), p. 174.

4   See Robert Campbell, Foreword, to *Boston Then and Now* by Peter Vanderwarker (New York: Dover, 1982), p. i.

5   Rudolf Arnheim, *The Dynamics of Architectural Form* (Berkeley: University of California Press, 1977), p. 131.

6   Peter F. Smith, *The Dynamics of Urbanism* (London: Hutchinson, 1974), p. 191.

7   Gordon Cullen, *The Concise Townscape* (New York: Van Nostrand Reinhold, 1976), p. 63; Kevin Lynch, *The Image of the City* (Cambridge: M.I.T. Press, 1960), p. 105.

8   Lawrence Halprin, *Cities* (Cambridge: M.I.T. Press, 1972), p. 51.

9   Kent C. Bloomer and Charles W. Moore, *Body, Memory, and Architecture* (New Haven: Yale University Press, 1977), p. 34; Raymond J. Curran, *Architecture and the Urban Experience* (New York: Van Nostrand Reinhold, 1976), p. 141.

10   Tadahiko Higuchi, *The Visual and Spatial Structure of Landscapes* (Cambridge: M.I.T. Press, 1983), p. 12.

11   Roger Scruton, *The Aesthetics of Architecture* (Princeton: Princeton University Press, 1979), p. 226; Norberg-Schultz, *Genius Loci*, p. 42.

12   Norberg-Schultz, *Genius Loci*, p. 42.

13   Halprin, *Cities*, p. 9; James Barker, Michael W. Fazin, and Hank Hildebrandt, *The Small Town as Art Object* ([Starkville, Miss.], 1975), p. 58; Jay Appleton, *The Experience of Landscape* (London: Wiley, 1975), p. 135; Cullen, *Concise Landscape*, p. 77.

14   Barrie B. Greenbie, *Spaces: Dimensions of the Human Landscape* (New Haven: Yale University Press, 1981), p. 119; Barker, Fazin, and Hildebrandt, *Small Town as Art Object*, p. 12.

15   Scruton, *Aesthetics of Architecture*, pp. 61–62.

16   Nairn, *American Landscape*, pp. 12, 43, 114; Bloomer and Moore, *Body, Memory, and Architecture*, p. 98.

17   Norberg-Schultz, *Genius Loci*, p. 42.

18   Peter F. Smith, *Architecture and the Human Dimension* (Westfield, N.J.: Eastview, 1979), p. 49.

19   Ibid., p. 183; Niels Prak, *The Visual Perception of the Built Environment* (Delft, Netherlands: Delft University Press, 1977), p. 23.

20   Robert Venturi, Denise S. Brown, and Steven Izenour, "Learning from Las Vegas," in *Environment and Cognition*, ed. William Ittleson (New York: Seminar Press, 1973), p. 108.

21   Nairn, *American Landscape*, p. 43; Arnheim, *Dynamics of Architectural Form*, p. 22.

22   Grady Clay, *Close-up: How to Read the American City* (New York: Praeger, 1973), p. 148.

23   Campbell, Foreword to Vanderwarker, *Boston Then and Now*, p. i; Norberg-Schultz, *Genius Loci*, p. 179.

24   Arnheim, *Dynamics of Architectural Form*, p. 134.

25   Higuchi, *Visual and Spatial Structure of Landscapes*, p. 47.

26   Curran, *Architecture and the Urban Experience*, pp. 126, 82.

27   Gyorgy Kepes, *Language of Vision* (Chicago: Theobald, 1969), p. 134.

28   Ibid., p. 143.

29   Waldron Faulkner, *Architecture and Color* (New York: Wiley Interscience, 1972), p. 5.

30   See John Hedgecoe, *The Art of Color Photography* (New York: Simon and Schuster, 1978), p. 56; Friedrich Schmuck, "Color Systems," in *Color in Townscape,* ed. Martina Duttmann, Friedrich Schmuck, and Johannes Uhl, trans. John W. Gabriel (San Francisco: Freeman, 1981), p. 59.

31   Kepes, *Language of Vision*, p. 141.

32   Hedgecoe, *Art of Color Photography*, p. 23.

33 Ibid., pp. 60–62; Paul D. Spreiregen, *Urban Design: The Architecture of Towns and Cities* (New York: McGraw-Hill, 1965), p. 77.

34 Faber Birren, *Light, Color, and Environment* (New York: Van Nostrand, 1969), p. 29; Duttmann, Schmuck, and Uhl, *Color in Townscape*, p. 99; Spreiregen, *Urban Design*, p. 76.

35 Duttmann, Schmuck, and Uhl, *Color in Townscape*, p. 111.

36 Birren, *Light, Color, and Environment*, p. 29.

37 Duttmann, Schmuck, and Uhl, *Color in Townscape*, pp. 86–88.

38 Kenneth E. Foote, *Color in Public Spaces: Toward a Communication-Based Theory of the Urban Built Environment* (Chicago: University of Chicago, Department of Geography, Research Paper no. 205, 1983), p. 1.

39 Duttmann, Schmuck, and Uhl, *Color in Townscape*, p. 42.

40 Norberg-Schultz, *Genius Loci*, p. 40.

41 Arnheim, *Dynamics of Architectural Form*, p. 25.

42 Kevin Lynch, *What Time Is This Place?* (Cambridge: M.I.T. Press, 1972), p. 65.

43 Ibid., p. 174.

44 Kevin Lynch, *Managing the Sense of a Region* (Cambridge: M.I.T. Press, 1976), p. 109. See also Irwin Altmann, *The Environment and Social Behavior* (Monterey, Calif.: Brooks-Cole, 1975) and Erving Goffman, *The Presentation of Self in Everyday Life* (Garden City, N.Y.: Doubleday Anchor, 1959).

45 Lynch, *What Time Is This Place?* p. 62.

5 LANDSCAPE AS VISUAL COMPOSITION

1 John A. Kouwenhoven, *Half a Truth Is Better than None: Some Unsystematic Conjectures about Art, Disorder, and American Experience* (Chicago: University of Chicago Press, 1982), p. 26.

2 Ibid., p. 28.

3 Martina Duttmann, "Color Sense and Color Scene," in *Color in Townscape*, ed. Martina Duttmann, Friedrich Schmuck, and Johannes Uhl, trans. John W. Gabriel (San Francisco: Freeman, 1981), p. 32.

4 Grady Clay, *Close-up: How to Read the American City* (New York: Praeger, 1973), p. 23.

5 Thomas Munro, *Form and Style in the Arts: An Introduction to Aesthetic Morphology* (Cleveland: Press of Case Western Reserve University, 1970), p. 344.

6 Kenneth Clark, *Landscape into Art* (New York: Harper and Row, 1949), p. 128; Barbara Novak, *Nature and Culture: American Landscape and Painting, 1825–1875* (New York: Oxford University Press, 1980), p. 228.

7 Clark, *Landscape into Art*, pp. 129–30.

8 Munro, *Form and Style*, p. 344; Clark, *Landscape into Art*, pp. 129–30.

9 Norman Battershill, *Light on Landscape* (London: Pittman, 1977), pp. 49–50.

10 John Szarkowski, quoted in ibid., p. 192.

11 Susan Sontag, *On Photography* (New York: Farrar, Straus and Giroux, 1977), p. 97.

12 Ibid., p. 138; John Hedgecoe, *The Art of Color Photography* (New York: Simon and Schuster, 1978), p. 64.

13 Donis A. Dondis, *A Primer of Visual Literacy* (Cambridge: M.I.T. Press, 1973), p. 7.

14 Sontag, *On Photography*, pp. 9–11, 24.

15 H. R. Poore, *Pictorial Composition and the Critical Judgement of Pictures* (New York: Putnam, 1903), p. 19.

16 Dondis, *Primer*, p. 114; Donald L. Weismann, *The Visual Arts as Human Experience* (Englewood Cliffs, N.J.: Prentice-Hall, 1970), p. 60.

17 Munro, *Form and Style*, p. 140.

18 Ibid., p. 15.

19 Gordon Cullen, *The Concise Townscape* (New York: Van Nostrand Reinhold, 1976), p. 33.

20 Dondis, *Primer*, p. 22.

21 Ibid., p. 84.

22 Poore, *Pictorial Composition*, p. 26.

23 Richard A. Rathbone, *Introduction to Functional Design* (New York: McGraw-Hill, 1950), p. 201.

24 Poore, *Pictorial Composition*, p. 26.

25 See Charles Bouleau, *The Painter's Secret Geometry: A Study of Composition in Art* (New York: Harcourt, Brace and World, 1963).

26 Dondis, *Primer*, p. 30.

27 Kevin Lynch, *The Image of the City* (Cambridge: M.I.T. Press, 1960), p. 2.

28 An analogy may be drawn from the study of architecture. See Rudolf Arnheim, *The Dynamics of Architectural Form* (Berkeley: University of California Press, 1977), p. 130.

29 Lynch, *Image of the City*, p. 106.

30 Jay Appleton, *The Experience of Landscape* (London: Wiley, 1975), p. 119. See also Arnheim, *The Dynamics of Architectural Form*, p. 76.

31 Lynch, *Image of the City*, pp. 47–48.

32 Ibid.

33 Donald Preziosi, *Architecture, Language and Meaning* (The Hague: Mouton, 1979), p. 16.

34 Ian C. Laurie, "Visual Aspects of Landscape Evaluation," in *The Aesthetics of Landscape*, ed. Jay Appleton (Didcot, U.K.: Rural Planning Services, 1980), pp. 80–81.

35 George Santayana, *The Sense of Beauty: Being the Outline of Aesthetic Theory* (New York: Collier Books, 1961), p. 99.

6 LANDSCAPE VISUALIZATION AND COGNITIVE MAPPING

1 See Roger M. Downs and David Stea, *Maps in Minds: Reflections on Cognitive Mapping* (New York: Harper and Row, 1977), p. 41.

2 Stephen Kaplan, "On Knowing the Environment," in *Human-scape: Environments for People,* ed. Stephen Kaplan and Rachel Kaplan (North Scituate, Mass.: Duxbury, 1978), p. 55.

3 David Canter, *The Psychology of Place* (London: Architectural Press, 1977), p. 77.

4 Dean MacCannell, *The Tourist: A New Theory of the Leisure Class* (New York: Schocken, 1976), p. 50. Also see Clare Gunn, *Vacationscapes: Designing Tourist Regions* (Austin: Bureau of Business Research, University of Texas, 1972).

5 Downs and Stea, *Maps in Minds,* p. 124.

6 James J. Gibson, *The Ecological Approach to Visual Perception* (Boston: Houghton Mifflin, 1979), pp. 199–200.

7 Ibid.

8 G. A. Kelly, *The Psychology of Personal Constructs* (New York: Norton, 1955); Amos Rapoport, *Human Aspects of Urban Form* (Oxford: Pergamon, 1977), p. 130.

9 Max Kaplan, *Leisure in America: A Social Inquiry* (New York: Wiley, 1960), p. 215.

10 Eric Cohen, "A Phenomenology of Tourist Experiences," *Sociology* 13 (1979): 192.

11 John L. Crompton, "Motivation for Pleasure Vacation," *Annals of Tourism Research* 6 (1979): 415. See also Kenneth Craik, "Human Responsiveness to Landscape: An Environmental Psychological Perspective," in *Response to Environment* (Raleigh: Student Publications of the School of Design, vol. 18, North Carolina State University, 1969), pp. 170–93.

12 Daniel Boorstin, *The Image: A Guide to Pseudo-Events* (New York: Harper Colophon, 1964), p. 116.

13 MacCannell, *Tourist,* p. 51.

14 Canter, *Psychology of Place,* p. 98.

15 Jerome Bruner, "On Perceptual Readiness," *Psychological Review* 64 (1957): 123–52; see esp. 146.

16 Canter, *Psychology of Place,* p. 31.

17 Gibson, *Ecological Approach,* p. 198.

18 Raymond J. Curran, *Architecture and the Urban Experience* (New York: Van Nostrand Reinhold, 1983), p. 61.

19 See Richard S. Wurman, *Making the City Observable* (Cambridge: M.I.T. Press, 1971).

20 Jan Mukarovsky, "On the Problem of Functions in Architecture," in *Structure, Sign, and Function: Selected Writings of Jan Mukarovsky,* ed. J. Burbank and P. Steiner (New Haven: Yale University Press, 1978).

21 See Donald Appleyard, "Why Buildings Are Known: A Predictive Tool for Architects and Planners," *Environment and Behavior* 1 (1969): 131–56, and Stephen Carr and Dale Schissler, "The City as a Trip: Perceptual Selection and Memory in the View from the Road," *Environment and Behavior* 1 (1969): 7–35.

22 Rudolf Arnheim, *The Dynamics of Architectural Form* (Berkeley: University of California Press, 1977), p. 205.

23 See John A. Jakle, *The American Small Town: Twentieth-Century Place Images* (Hamden, Conn.: Archon Books, 1982), p. 5.

24 Canter, *Psychology of Place,* p. 30.

7 CONCLUSION

1 Barry Sadler and Allen Carlson, "Environmental Aesthetics in Interdisciplinary Perspective," in *Environmental Aesthetics: Essays in Interpretation,* ed. Barry Sadler and Allen Carlson (Victoria: University of Victoria, Department of Geography, Western Geographical Series, vol. 20, 1982), p. 3; Jay Appleton, *The Experience of Landscape* (London: Wiley, 1975).

2 Appleton, *Experience of Landscape,* pp. 70–74.

3 Lawrence Durrell, *Spirit of Place: Letters and Essays on Travel,* ed. Allan G. Thomas (New York: Dutton, 1969); Christian Norberg-Schultz, *Genius Loci: Towards a Phenomenology of Architecture* (New York: Rizzoli, 1980); Yi-Fu Tuan, *Topophilia: A Study of Environmental Perception, Attitudes, and Values* (Englewood Cliffs, N.J.: Prentice-Hall, 1974).

4 Kevin Lynch, *The Image of the City* (Cambridge: M.I.T. Press, 1960).

5 David Lowenthal, "The Pioneer Landscape: An American Dream," *Great Plains Quarterly* 21 (1982): 5–19.

6 See Dean MacCannell, *The Tourist: A New Theory of the Leisure Class* (New York: Schocken, 1976); Foster R. Dulles, *America Learns to Play: A History of Recreation* (New York: Appleton-Century-Crofts, 1965); Max Kaplan, *Leisure in America: A Social Inquiry* (New York: Wiley, 1960).

7 David Lowenthal and Hugh C. Prince, "English Landscape Tastes," *Geographical Review* 55 (1965): 186–222.

8 See Thomas S. Kuhn, *The Structure of Scientific Revolutions* (Chicago: University of Chicago Press, 1970).

9 For discussion of behavioral research and environmental design, see Constance Perin, *With Man in Mind: An Interdisciplinary Prospectus for Environmental Design* (Cambridge: M.I.T. Press, 1970); David Canter, *The Psychology of Place* (London: Architectural Press, 1977).

10 George Santayana, *The Sense of Beauty: Being the Outline of Aesthetic Theory* (New York: Colliers, 1961), p. 99; Lynch, *Image of the City,* p. 2.

11 D. W. Meinig, "Environmental Appreciation: Localities as a Humane Art," *Western Humanities Review* 25 (Winter, 1971): 6.

Selected
Bibliography

Altmann, Irwin. *The Environment and Social Behavior.* Monterey, Calif.: Brooks-Cole, 1975.

Appleton, Jay. *The Experience of Landscape.* London: Wiley, 1975.

———. "Pleasure and the Perception of Habitat." In *Environmental Aesthetics: Essays in Interpretation,* edited by Barry Sadler and Allen Carlson, pp. 27–45. Victoria: University of Victoria, Department of Geography, Western Geographical Series, vol. 20, 1982.

Appleyard, Donald. "Why Buildings Are Known: A Predictive Tool for Architects and Planners." *Environment and Behavior* 1 (1969): 131–56.

Appleyard, Donald, Kevin Lynch, and John R. Meyer. *The View from the Road.* Cambridge: M.I.T. Press, 1963.

Arnheim, Rudolf. *The Dynamics of Architectural Form.* Berkeley: University of California Press, 1977.

———. *Visual Thinking.* Berkeley: University of California Press, 1969.

Ashihara, Yoshinobu. *The Aesthetic Townscape,* translated by Lynne E. Riggs. Cambridge: M.I.T. Press, 1983.

Barker, James F., Michael W. Fazin, and Hank Hildebrandt. *The Small Town as Art Object.* [Starkville, Miss.], 1975.

Barker, Roger G. *Ecological Psychology*. Stanford: Stanford University Press, 1968.

Battershill, Norman. *Light on Landscape*. London: Pittman, 1977.

Beck, Robert. "Spatial Meaning and the Properties of the Environment." In *Environmental Perception and Behavior,* edited by David Lowenthal, pp. 18–41. Chicago: University of Chicago, Department of Geography, Research Paper no. 109, 1967.

Birren, Faber. *Light, Color, and Environment*. New York: Van Nostrand, 1969.

Bloomer, Kent C., and Charles W. Moore. *Body, Memory, and Architecture*. New Haven: Yale University Press, 1977.

Boorstin, Daniel. *The Image: A Guide to Pseudo-Events*. New York: Harper Colophon, 1964.

Bouleau, Charles. *The Painter's Secret Geometry: A Study of Composition in Art*. New York: Harcourt, Brace and World, 1963.

Broadbent, Geoffrey, Richard Bunt, and Tomas Llorens, eds. *Meaning and Behavior in the Built Environment*. Chichester: Wiley, 1980.

Bruner, Jerome. "On Perceptual Readiness." *Psychological Review* 64 (1957): 123–52.

Campbell, Robert. Foreword, to *Boston Then and Now,* by Peter Vanderwarker. New York: Dover, 1982.

Canby, Henry S. "Traveling Intelligently in America." In *Essays of Today (1926–1927),* edited by Odell Shepard and Robert Hillyer, pp. 166–79. New York: Century, 1928.

Canter, David. *The Psychology of Place*. London: Architectural Press, 1977.

Carr, Stephen, and Dale Schissler. "The City as a Trip: Perceptual Selection and Memory in the View from the Road." *Environment and Behavior* 1 (1969): 7–35.

Clark, Kenneth. *Landscape Into Art*. New York: Harper and Row, 1949.

———. *Looking at Pictures*. New York: Holt, Rinehart, and Winston, 1960.

Clay, Grady. *Close-up: How to Read the American City*. New York: Praeger, 1973.

Cohen, Eric. "A Phenomenology of Tourist Experiences." *Sociology* 13 (1979): 108–201.

Cosgrove, Denis E. *Social Formation and Symbolic Landscape*. London: Croom Helm, 1984.

Craik, Kenneth. "Human Responsiveness to Landscape: An Environmental Psychological Perspective." In *Response to Environment,* pp. 170–93. Raleigh: Student Publications of the School of Design, Vol. 18, North Carolina State University, 1969.

Crompton, John L. "Motivation for Pleasure Vacation." *Annals of Tourism Research* 6 (1979): 408–23.

Cullen, Gordon. *The Concise Townscape*. New York: Van Nostrand Reinhold, 1976.

Curran, Raymond J. *Architecture and the Urban Experience.* New York: Van Nostrand Reinhold, 1983.

Day, R. H. *Human Perception.* Sydney: Wiley, 1969.

De Bono, E. *The Mechanism of Mind.* London: Cape, 1969.

Donat, John, ed. *World Architecture 4.* London: Studio Vista, 1967.

Dondis, Donis A. *A Primer of Visual Literacy.* Cambridge: M.I.T. Press, 1973.

Downs, Roger M., and David Stea. *Maps in Minds: Reflections on Cognitive Mapping.* New York: Harper and Row, 1977.

Dreyfuss, Henry. *The Measure of Man: Human Factors in Design.* New York: Whitney Publications, 1959.

Dulles, Foster R. *America Learns to Play: A History of Recreation.* New York: Appleton–Century–Crofts, 1965.

Durrell, Lawrence. *Spirit of Place: Letters and Essays on Travel.* Edited by Allan G. Thomas. New York: Dutton, 1969.

Duttmann, Martina. "Color Sense and Color Scene." In *Color in Townscape,* edited by Martina Duttmann, Friedrich Schmuck, and Johannes Uhl, translated by John W. Gabriel. San Francisco: Freeman, 1981.

Ewart, John. "Art Environment and Education." In *The Aesthetics of Landscape,* edited by Jay Appleton, pp. 90–93. Didcot, U.K.: Rural Planning Services, 1980.

Faulkner, Waldron. *Architecture and Color.* New York: Wiley Interscience, 1972.

Foote, Kenneth E. *Color in Public Spaces: Toward a Communication-Based Theory of the Urban Built Environment.* Chicago: University of Chicago, Department of Geography, Research Paper no. 205, 1983.

Gibson, James J. *The Ecological Approach to Visual Perception.* Boston: Houghton Mifflin, 1979.

———. *The Perception of the Visual World.* Boston: Houghton Mifflin, 1950.

Goffman, Erving. *The Presentation of Self in Everyday Life.* Garden City, N.Y.: Doubleday Anchor, 1959.

Golledge, Reginald G., Terrence R. Smith, James W. Pellegrino, Sally Doherty, and Sandra R. Marshall. "A Conceptual Model and Empirical Analysis of Children's Acquisitions of Spatial Knowledge." *Journal of Environmental Psychology* 5 (1985): 125–52.

Greenbie, Barrie B. *Spaces: Dimensions of the Human Landscape.* New Haven: Yale University Press, 1981.

Gunn, Clare. *Vacationscapes: Designing Tourist Regions.* Austin: Bureau Business Research, University of Texas, 1972.

Halprin, Lawrence. *Cities.* Cambridge: M.I.T. Press, 1972.

———. *Freeways.* New York: Reinhold, 1966.

Hart, Roger. *Children's Experience of Place.* New York: Irvington, 1978.

Hartshorn, Richard. *The Nature of Geography.* Lancaster, Penn.: Association of American Geographers, 1939.

Hedgecoe, John. *The Art of Color Photography*. New York: Simon and Schuster, 1978.

Higuchi, Tadahiko. *The Visual and Spatial Structure of Landscapes*. Cambridge: M.I.T. Press, 1983.

Ittleson, William H. *Visual Space Perception*. New York: Springer, 1960.

—————, ed. *Environment and Cognition*. New York: Seminar Press, 1973.

Jackson, John B. *Discovering the Vernacular Landscape*. New Haven: Yale University Press, 1984.

Jakle, John A. *The American Small Town: Twentieth-Century Place Images*. Hamden, Conn.: Archon Books, 1982.

—————. *The Tourist: Travel in Twentieth-Century North America*. Lincoln: University of Nebraska Press, 1984.

Johnson, Hildegard B., and Gerald R. Pitzl. "Viewing and Perceiving the Rural Scene: Visualization in Human Geography." *Progress in Human Geography* 5 (1981): 211–33.

Jung, Carl G. *Seelenproblem Der Gegenwart*. Zurich: Rascher, 1931.

Kaplan, Max. *Leisure in America: A Social Inquiry*. New York: Wiley, 1960.

Kaplan, Stephen, and Rachel Kaplan. *Cognition and Environment: Functioning in an Uncertain World*. New York: Praeger, 1982.

—————, eds. *Humanscape: Environment for People*. North Scituate, Mass.: Duxbury, 1978.

Kaufman, Lloyd. *Perception: The World Transformed*. New York: Oxford University Press, 1979.

Kelly, G. A. *The Psychology of Personal Constructs*. New York: Norton, 1955.

Kepes, Gyorgy. *Language of Vision*. Chicago: Theobald, 1969.

Kouwenhoven, John A. *Half a Truth Is Better Than None: Some Unsystematic Conjectures about Art, Disorder, and American Experience*. Chicago: University of Chicago Press, 1982.

Krampen, M. *Meaning in the Urban Environment*. London: Pion, 1979.

Kuhn, Thomas S. *The Structure of Scientific Revolutions*. Chicago: University of Chicago Press, 1970.

Laurie, Ian C. "Visual Aspects of Landscape Evaluation." In *The Aesthetics of Landscape,* edited by Jay Appleton. Didcot, U.K.: Rural Planning Services, 1980.

Litton, R. Burton, Jr. *Forest Landscape Description and Inventories*. N.p.: USDA Forest Service Research Paper, PSW–49, 1968.

Lowenthal, David. "Finding Valued Landscapes." *Progress in Human Geography* 2 (1978): 373–410.

—————. "The Pioneer Landscape: An American Dream." *Great Plains Quarterly* 21 (1982): 5–19.

Lowenthal, David, and Hugh C. Prince. "English Landscape Tastes." *Geographical Review* 55 (1965): 186–222.

Lynch, Kevin. *The Image of the City*. Cambridge: M.I.T. Press, 1960.

—————. *Managing the Sense of a Region*. Cambridge: M.I.T. Press, 1976.

————. *What Time Is This Place?* Cambridge: M.I.T. Press, 1972.

MacCannell, Dean. *The Tourist: A New Theory of the Leisure Class.* New York: Schocken, 1976.

Meinig, D. W. "Environmental Appreciation: Localities as a Humane Art." *Western Humanities Review* 25 (1971): 1–11.

————, ed. *The Interpretation of Ordinary Landscapes.* New York: Oxford University Press, 1979.

Morris, C. *Signs, Language, and Behavior.* New York: Braziller, 1955.

Mukarovsky, Jan. "On the Problem of Functions in Architecture." In *Structure, Sign, and Function: Selected Writings of Jan Mukarovsky,* edited by J. Burbank and P. Steiner. New Haven: Yale University Press, 1978.

Munro, Thomas. *Form and Style in the Arts: An Introduction to Aesthetic Morphology.* Cleveland: Press of Case Western Reserve University, 1970.

Nairn, Ian. *The American Landscape: A Critical View.* New York: Random House, 1965.

Nassauer, Joan. "A Non-Linear Model of Visual Quality." *Landscape Research* 5 (1980): 29–31.

Norberg-Schultz, Christian. *Genius Loci: Towards a Phenomenology of Architecture.* New York: Rizzoli, 1980.

Novak, Barbara. *Nature and Culture: American Landscape Painting, 1825–1875.* New York: Oxford University Press, 1980.

Passini, Romedi. "Spatial Representations, A Wayfinding Perspective." *Journal of Environmental Psychology* 4 (1984): 153–64.

Penning-Rowsell, Edmund C. "Fluctuating Fortunes in Gauging Landscape Value." *Progress in Human Geography* 5 (1981): 25–41.

Perin, Constance. *With Man in Mind: An Interdisciplinary Prospectus for Environmental Design.* Cambridge: M.I.T. Press, 1970.

Piaget, Jean, and Barbel Inhelder. *The Child's Conception of Space.* Translated by F. J. Langdon and J. L. Lunzer. New York: Norton, 1967.

Pickles, John. *Phenomenology, Science and Geography: Spatiality and the Human Sciences.* Cambridge: Cambridge University Press, 1985.

Pocock, Douglas, and Ray Hudson. *Images of the Urban Environment.* New York: Columbia University Press, 1978.

Poore, H. R. *Pictorial Composition and the Critical Judgement of Pictures.* New York: Putnam, 1903.

Porteous, Douglas. "Approaches to Environmental Aesthetics." *Journal of Environmental Psychology* 2 (1982): 53–66.

Prak, Niels. *The Visual Perception of the Built Environment.* Delft, Netherlands: Delft University Press, 1977.

Preziosi, Donald. *Architecture, Language and Meaning.* The Hague: Mouton, 1979.

Rapoport, Amos. *Human Aspects of Urban Form.* Oxford: Pergamon Press, 1977.

————. *The Meaning of the Built Environment: A Nonverbal Communication Approach.* Beverly Hills, Calif.: Sage, 1982.

Rapoport, Amos, and Ron Hawkes. "The Perception of Urban

Complexity." *American Institute of Planners Journal* 36 (1970): 106–11.

Rathbone, Richard A. *Introduction to Functional Design*. New York: McGraw-Hill, 1950.

Relph, E. *Place and Placelessness*. London: Pion, 1976.

Sadler, Barry, and Allen Carlson. "Environmental Aesthetics in Interdisciplinary Perspective." In *Environmental Aesthetics: Essays in Interpretation,* edited by Barry Sadler and Allen Carlson, pp. 1–5. Victoria: University of Victoria, Department of Geography, Western Geographical Series, vol. 20, 1982.

Santayana, George. *The Sense of Beauty: Being the Outline of Aesthetic Theory*. New York: Collier Books, 1961.

Schmuck, Friedrich. "Color Systems." In *Color in Townscape,* edited by Martina Duttmann, Friedrich Schmuck, and Johannes Uhl, translated by John W. Gabriel. San Francisco: Freeman, 1981.

Scruton, Roger. *The Aesthetics of Architecture*. Princeton: Princeton University Press, 1979.

Seaman, David. "The Phenomenological Contribution to Environmental Psychology." *Journal of Environmental Psychology* 2 (1982): 119–40.

Segall, William H., Donald T. Campbell, and Melville J. Herskovits. *The Influence of Culture on Visual Perception*. Indianapolis: Bobbs-Merrill, 1966.

Smith, Peter F. *Architecture and the Human Dimension*. Westfield, N.J.: Eastview, 1979.

———. *The Dynamics of Urbanism*. London: Hutchinson, 1974.

———. *The Syntax of Cities*. London: Hutchinson, 1977.

Sontag, Susan. *On Photography*. New York: Farrar, Straus, and Giroux, 1977.

Spreiregen, Paul D. *Urban Design: The Architecture of Towns and Cities*. New York: McGraw-Hill, 1965.

Thornberg, Jose M. "Towards an Epistemology of Architectural Design as a Place-Making Activity." In *Meaning and Behavior in the Built Environment,* edited by Geoffrey Broadbent, Richard Bunt, and Tomas Llorens, pp. 183–94. Chichester: Wiley, 1980.

Tuan, Yi-Fu. *Space and Place: The Perspective of Experience*. Minneapolis: University of Minnesota Press, 1977.

———. *Topophilia: A Study of Environmental Perception, Attitudes, and Values*. Englewood Cliffs, N.J.: Prentice-Hall, 1974.

Ulrich, R. "Visual Landscapes and Psychological Well-Being." *Landscape Research* 4 (1979): 17–23.

Venturi, Robert, Denise S. Brown, and Steven Izenour. *Learning from Las Vegas: The Forgotten Symbolism of Architectural Form*. Cambridge: M.I.T. Press, 1977.

Weismann, Donald L. *The Visual Arts as Human Experience*. Englewood Cliffs, N.J.: Prentice-Hall, 1970.

Wurman, Raymond. *Making the City Observable*. Cambridge: M.I.T. Press, 1971.

Zube, Ervin H., James L. Sell, and Jonathan G. Taylor. "Landscape Perception: Research, Application, and Theory." *Landscape Planning* 9 (1982): 1–33.

Index